NATURAL DYEING

NATURAL DYEING

Learn How to Create Colour and Dye Textiles Naturally

Kathryn Davey

PHOTOGRAPHY BY
Doreen Kilfeather & Kathryn Davey

Hardie Grant

BOOKS

CONTENTS

INTRODUCTION

I fell into natural dyeing almost accidentally, having never studied textiles or natural dyeing formally. Through books and from dyers who generously shared what they knew, I learnt through trial and error and a desire to understand. It became clear that there were no mistakes in this process: every result was a necessary and beautiful step along the way.

When it comes to natural dyes, indigo was my first true love. Like all firsts it left an indelible impression on me and I was completely enamoured, obsessed and consumed with the beauty and range of just one colour, blue. And so it continued with every new dye I began to work with. They each held their own particular magic, their aroma when brewing, the colours and how they reacted when modified slightly. What struck me deeply was how complementary the tones of natural dyes were with each other. How you could take one dye and change it ever so slightly to give you a whole new range of variations. They were soft, gentle, soothing and beautiful like nothing I had seen before. The possibilities were and still are truly endless.

At first I took it in bite-sized chunks. I would begin with a new dye and experiment until I understood its palette and nuances. It was incredible to see that nature held an array of colour within its fibres, almost like a secret or hidden language of colour, waiting to be coaxed forth. I became fascinated by the alchemy of dyeing and the more I learnt, the more humbling and deeply satisfying the process became. I remember how it felt to learn something new; the intense desire to get to a certain place of familiarity and comfort, to work through the feeling of being overwhelmed and lack knowledge. There is something quite beautiful about not only beginning but being a beginner in something that interests you.

In many ways natural dyeing is similar to cooking. There is an alchemy that happens. I know how it feels to create a dish I have prepared a thousand times and how different it feels to follow a recipe for the first time. It is this feeling of unfamiliarity and lack of confidence that I want to help others overcome when learning how to work with plant dyes.

Natural dyeing is one of the most labour-intensive endeavours I have tried, next to parenting. It requires copious amounts of time and patience. You have to be willing to invest many hours of work with no solid guarantee of a result. Working with natural dyes is something I never grow tired of, and lately I am coming to appreciate how cathartic it is for myself and many others who work with plant dyes and colour in this way.

What began from a place of intrigue and curiosity, developed into a borderline addiction and obsession. I fell down the most beautiful rabbit hole into a world of colour and unlimited possibilities. Plant dyes teach me about colour in a way that nothing else has. They have expanded my appreciation and increased my respect for the natural world while delighting my senses and soothing my soul.

With this book, I want to share what I have learnt in a simple and easily digested way. There are many ways to work with plant dyes and I encourage you to find your own. It is my hope that experimenting with natural dyes will be as beautiful, peaceful, enjoyable and as deeply satisfying for you as it has been for me.

Natural Dyeing & Its Many Benefits

Natural dyeing is an ancient practice of extracting colour or dyes from plants, invertebrates or minerals for the purpose of dyeing cloth and natural fibres. We do not know the exact point in history when our ancestors discovered that natural materials could be used as forms of pigment, ink or dye, but there is evidence of mineral-based pigments used to depict scenes of everyday life in the earliest known cave paintings.

While we suspect that cooking and other daily practices may have informed the discovery of food and plants as dyestuff, we can be more certain how and when it first began. We know that natural dyes have been used to colour textiles for at least 6,000 years. With many vibrant examples of preserved textiles, garments and rugs from the ancient world we have learnt much about the history of our previous civilisations and their relationship to natural colour. Long before synthetic dyes were discovered, natural dyes were the sole method of colouring fibre and cloth. As civilisations began to grow and expand, trade routes opened up and dyes were shared around the world. Natural dyeing was practised throughout Greece, Rome, Egypt, South America, Africa and Asia and among the native people of North America. When synthetic dyes were discovered in the mid-nineteenth century, they were quickly adopted as the main source of commercial dye as they were both cheaper to develop and considerably less labour-intensive to produce. With the development of the synthetic dye industry, natural dyes became secondary and so began the demise of the natural dyeing market.

Working With Nature

Once you begin working with plant dyes you start to learn about the many sources of colour available to us through the natural world. By working with plants, flowers, trees or food waste it opens you up to a new relationship with nature, one of appreciation, curiosity and respect. The process of extracting colour naturally can be an enjoyable experience. The possibilities of natural dyes lie in the subtlety and range of colours alone, modified or combined with each other. These dyes have an innate beauty and life to them that are lacking in synthetic dyes. Plant dyes make you look at the natural world around you in a different light. Once you start dyeing you begin to look at things, not only to appreciate the innate beauty of what they are, but also to see the colour that lies behind each seed, plant, leaf, tree or root.

Discover the Colour All Around You

It becomes fascinating to see that there is so much colour available to use through the natural world. A garden full of dandelions is no longer a garden full of weeds, but full of greens and yellows. A cup of tea or coffee, breakfast, a meal, all hold potential for colour. Colour is dormant in so many aspects of our lives. Take waste, for instance, it can be transformed into something beautiful to dye textiles with. There is something so magical and fluid about the quality of natural dyes and how they catch the light in different ways. Synthetic dyes are flat and one dimensional whereas the tones of natural dyes reflect light differently, they dance and come alive before your eyes. They, like all things in nature, change throughout the light of the day and through the life of the textiles they colour.

Working with plant dyes connects you to the seasons of nature, to the tree that flowers in spring, gives fruit in summer and seed in autumn, all yielding different colours for the dye pot depending on the time of the year. In the most unassuming way working with plant dyes creates a relationship to nature, one of observation, appreciation and respect.

Slowing Down and Being Creative

As we all go through our lives, one thing is certain, creative outlets are essential to our mental health and well-being. The simple act of slowing down and working with our hands calms the mind. Allowing ourselves to take time to create and explore what

'In every walk with nature one receives far more than he seeks.' John Muir

interests us outside the daily grind is an act of self-love and a huge gift to ourselves. The entire process – the gathering or foraging, cooking, the alchemy, the necessary patience and the beautiful end result – pulls you in and absorbs you fully, calming the body and occupying the mind. It is a deeply satisfying process of creating something beautiful from nature. It takes you into a world of colour that can soothe and nourish your soul. You cannot rush natural dyeing as every step in the process takes time. By its nature it is calming, grounding and meditative, forcing you to slow down and be present.

As we become more aware of the detrimental impact of fast fashion and industrialisation on the environment, and as a shift towards a more sustainable way of living occurs, making our own clothes, repairing the ones we have, and finding new ways to repurpose what we already own is becoming more important. It can be very satisfying to dye your own fibre whether to make your own clothes or just add beautifully coloured textiles into your life. Being able to take what you have and give it a new life by

dyeing with plants or food waste is a wonderful way to create a more sustainable future together.

Helping the Environment

Apart from the benefits to ourselves, natural dyeing is a wonderful way to show our respect and appreciation for the earth. Did you know that the fashion industry is the second biggest polluter after the oil industry? By gathering what is around you and using what you have, you are directly contributing to a better future for the earth. It is an environmentally safe and non-toxic way to develop colours naturally and to bring colour into our lives without harming the earth.

One of the wonderful things about natural dyeing is that a large part of it is exploratory. Although there are some guidelines and a few rules of thumb, much of it has to be learnt by practise and it is only with trial, beautiful error, experimentation and exploration that you will learn how to coax natural colour into your life.

Equipment & Considerations

One of the wonderful things about starting out as a natural dyer is that you don't have to spend money on expensive equipment or materials. All you need to begin is something to dye, water, a heat source, a cooking pot and some dye plants. You can begin, like I did, in your kitchen with what you have.

If you have a studio or extra space in your home you can set up a simple natural dyeing station or work bench. Wherever you decide to set up it is important to be able to work as freely as possible.

You can get away with doing this in your kitchen at first but if this is something you are going to pursue it would be ideal to have a separate space just for dyeing. It can be quite messy and it is nice to be able to work without having to worry about the mess you are making or the dye splatters across your walls.

As already mentioned, natural dyeing is like cooking and uses many of the same tools and equipment, some of which you will already own. If you are going to be sourcing tools from your kitchen, it is important to keep these separate from your regular kitchen equipment as you don't want any crossover. If you are working from your kitchen make sure you don't prepare or handle food while doing your natural dyeing. Always wipe up your spills and wash your work surfaces thoroughly once you are done.

Cooking pots The first thing you will need to get started are some cooking pots. I was lucky enough to get my hands on some of my mum's old aluminium pots. You can ask your friends and family and see if anyone has any old pots they don't use any more or go to second-hand or charity shops. If you are purchasing, I would recommend stainless steel as these are easier to clean. Ideally, you want your pots to be large enough so that the items you are dyeing have space to move freely. You don't want your fibres squashed up against the sides as this will create uneven and inconsistent results. With space being

the basic requirement, you will probably start small and work up in pot size as your confidence grows.

Heat source If you are working in your kitchen you can use your stove, but if you are working in a separate space then you will need to purchase a portable electric or gas stove. If you have electricity, an electric hob will be fine, but if your dye station is away from an electrical outlet, a gas stove might be your best solution. Make sure that whatever you set your hob on is sturdy and strong enough to hold the weight of the pots once they are filled with water.

Water source You will also need a water source. If you are working in your kitchen this won't be an issue. If you are working away from the house, you will need to be close enough to a water source and a drain to fill and empty your pots. Keep in mind that pots filled with water can be heavy so the closer you are to a water source, the easier it will be on your back.

Ventilation When working with natural dyes always work in a well-ventilated area. If you are working in your kitchen, keep the windows open and the extractor fan on. If you can't get good ventilation inside then set your pots up in a garage or sheltered space outside if possible. Some dyes release harmful vapours into the air so you will need to keep this in mind when setting up your dye station.

Other considerations When you go foraging you will need a pair of sharp scissors and something to collect your foraged plant materials. You will also need gloves, wooden spoons, tongs, sieves, containers and an eco-friendly detergent (see page 13).

Dyeing Equipment

Whisk

Tongs

Measuring spoon & jugs

Wooden spoons

Sieves or tea strainers

Washing line & pegs

Digital scales: for weighing powders & fibres

Electric or gas stove: if working outside the kitchen

Glass jars: for saving & storing dried materials & dye baths

Eco-friendly detergent or pH-neutral soap

Sharp scissors or secateurs

Pots: a selection in a variety of both small & large sizes, depending on what your are dyeing

Containers: for rinsing & soaking pieces

Bowls: I have some large enamel bowls that I use to hold my pieces straight from the dye bath

Jugs: for mixing, measuring & pouring

Rubber gloves: to protect your hands

Don't worry too much about buying everything in the list above. It has taken me a few years to build up my equipment and dye supplies. When you first get started just use what you already have and slowly add to your equipment as you go. Most of these can be bought inexpensively.

Powders

There are a few powders you will need to purchase if you are going to be doing this regularly. I will explain their uses in more detail in the following pages. You can get started with some basic dyeing without using these but they are essential if you want to build your skills and colour palette as a natural dyer.

Tannin powder (used as a 'mordant', sold as tannin or oak gall powder)

Potassium aluminium sulphate (used as a 'mordant' or for 'modifying' colour)

Soda ash (used for 'scouring' fibre or 'modifying' colour)

Detergents

Another important item to have in your toolbox is a pH-neutral soap, such as pure Castile liquid soap or an eco-friendly detergent. Quite often traditional soaps or detergents contain chemicals, perfumes or dyes that can affect the colour of many natural dyes. Some dyes are more sensitive to changes in pH than others so it will be more noticeable with certain dyes and not so much with others. When looking for an eco-friendly detergent, I recommend choosing an unperfumed, non-citrus kind if possible. Typically, washing-up liquid is pH-neutral so if you are having trouble finding a suitable detergent, you can use washing-up liquid in the interim.

UNDERSTANDING & CHOOSING FIBRE

When it comes to natural dyeing, it is always natural fibres that are used with plant dyes. And when it comes to natural fibre there are two main groups: animal and plant fibres. Animal fibres are made of protein and include fibres that come from an animal, such as wool, silk, alpaca or mohair. Plant or vegetable fibres are cellulose based and include anything that comes from a plant or is grown in the earth, such as cotton, flax, hemp or nettle.

It is important to understand the fibre you are working with in order to get the best results from your efforts. The two groups are treated differently in how they are 'scoured', 'mordanted' and dyed.

Fibres come in many forms. Typically, the material in its raw form is spun into fibre; at which point, it can be left in this form or woven into fabric. I use the term fibre throughout this book to refer to any of the natural fibres we work with whether it is silk, yarn, hair, raw fleece, unwoven plant fibres or fibre of either type. Whichever fibre you choose to work with will determine how you both prepare and dye your fibre.

Plant or Vegetable Fibres

Plant fibres are straightforward to work with and a great place to start as a natural dyer. Although animal fibres may absorb the dye more fully, plant fibres are hardier than animal fibres making them easier to work with when first familiarising yourself with the processes of natural dyeing. Plant fibres include cotton, linen, hemp or nettle. There are a few other plant fibres on the market but research shows that they are either grown destructively or require toxic chemicals in their manufacturing.

Animal Fibres

Animal fibres absorb natural dyes beautifully but they need to be dyed with care so as not to shrink and damage the fibre. You can apply heat to animal fibres but it needs to be done slowly and gradually. Any sudden or extreme changes in temperature will cause the fibres to contract and shrink, or felt, which unfortunately is irreversible. I'm not sure about you but I am quite familiar with that sinking feeling when a beloved wool piece is rendered unwearable, so exercise caution when dyeing wool or animal fibre. I always err on the safe side and cold dye or use very low temperatures when dyeing wool. Animal fibres include wool, silk, cashmere and alpaca.

Another thing to note is that fibre groups and types will take up dye in different ways. If you were to dye with silk, linen and cotton, each would take up the dye differently and would have a different quality to the colour.

When it comes to choosing fibres to dye with, try to source organic where possible. Ideally, you want fibre in as close to its natural state as possible, so unbleached or natural is always best. Do your research. Fibre that is consciously sourced will usually be traceable. Find out where your fibre is grown and what chemicals, if any, are used in the manufacturing process. How does the crop affect the land it is grown on? How are the people who work the land and weave the fibre treated and compensated? Find organisations, companies and individuals that are committed to reducing the carbon footprint through the supply chain of textiles. It is possible you will pay more for this type of fibre but it is better for the communities in which it is grown, the climate, the environment and ultimately for all of us.

Understanding Fibre

PLANT FIBRE

Cellulose or Vegetable Fibre
cotton, linen, nettle, hemp, etc.

- durable
- takes hot or cold temperature
- withstands sudden changes
  in temperature

SUITABLE DYEING METHOD
hot dyeing (see page 41)

ANIMAL FIBRE

Protein Fibre
wool, silk, alpaca, cashmere, etc.

- delicate
- suited to low temperature
- can't tolerate sudden changes
  in temperature

SUITABLE DYEING METHOD
cool dyeing (see page 40); solar dyeing (see page 41)

Preparing Your Fibre for Dyeing

One of the most important steps in natural dyeing begins long before you add your fibres to the dye pot. No matter what fibre you are using everything needs to be cleaned thoroughly prior to dyeing. We do this by a method known as scouring.

Natural fibres are often coated in naturally present waxes or oils. More often than not, chemicals and softening agents are added to fibre when it is being manufactured or woven into fabric. Scouring is a method of removing chemicals, oils or waxes from the fibre in order to make it possible for the dye to penetrate the fibre as fully and evenly as possible. If these impurities remain, they will stop the dye from soaking in fully and result in weak, inconsistent or blotchy results.

Traditionally, this was done in large pots filled with simmering water. The fibre was then added to the pot with sodium bicarbonate to remove all the impurities and heated gently until the water became murky. The water was drained off and the process repeated until the water ran clear. Today, we can do this much more conveniently by using a washing machine.

In order to scour effectively you will need to purchase soda ash or soda crystals for the plant fibres and soda ash or pH-neutral soap for animal fibres. You can buy soda ash from online dye supply stores or you can purchase soda crystals (or washing soda) from grocery stores or supermarkets.

How to Scour Plant Fibre: Convenient Method

1. Add about 200 g (7 oz) fibre or 2–3 small items to the washing machine, then add 1 tablespoon soda crystals (washing soda) or 1 teaspoon soda ash to the drawer. DO NOT ADD DETERGENT.

2. Run a lukewarm or cold cycle, I use a 40°C (104°F) cycle when washing plant fibres. If you normally wash your plant fibres at a higher temperature, please feel free to do so. For heavily soiled, previously worn or antique pieces, you may need to run them through a second cycle. When your fibre is scoured, dry and store it until you are ready to mordant and dye.

How to Scour Plant Fibre: Stove-top Method

1. Using a pot large enough to allow your fibre to move freely, fill three-quarters full with water and bring to a gentle boil.

2. In a separate container, dissolve 1 tablespoon soda crystals or 1 teaspoon soda ash in warm water. Add the dissolved crystals to the main pot of water and stir.

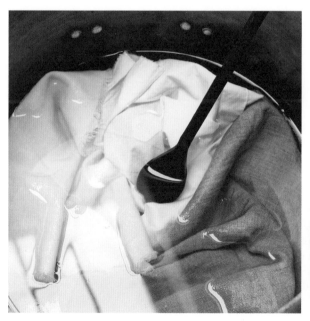

3. Place your fibre in the pot, removing any air bubbles. Reduce the heat to a low simmer and simmer for 1–2 hours, stirring the fibre every 20–30 minutes.

4. Turn off the heat and leave the water to cool. Remove your fibre from the pot, rinse and leave to dry.

How to Scour Animal Fibre

1. Fill a large container with cold water and add 1 tablespoon pH-neutral soap.

2. Add your fibre, removing any air and making sure it is completely submerged. Leave the fibre to soak overnight.

3. The next day, rinse until the fibre is free from any soapy residue.

4. Hang to dry or, if mordanting, place the fibre in a container of cold water.

A Few Points to Remember

Do not add detergent when scouring your fibre. Detergent will not be added until you have completed all the steps and finished dyeing your fibre.

Animal fibres cannot tolerate extreme or sudden changes in temperature, so never pour hot water straight onto animal fibres.

The importance of this step cannot be overlooked. I believe good scouring is the foundation of successful natural dyeing and creates consistent, even colours.

Note: Fibre labelled as PFD (prepared for dye) or RTD (ready to dye) is sold under the premise that it does not need to be scoured. It usually lacks the starches, softeners and optical whiteners found in many white fibres.

Understanding Mordanting

Once you have scoured your fibre, and before you create your dye bath, the fibre has to be treated with one additional step before being ready to dye. In order to assist the dye with binding or fixing to the fibre a substance known as a mordant has to be added.

Mordant comes from the Latin *mordere*, 'to bite', and is necessary for a number of reasons. It helps fix the dye to the fibre, increases colour fastness (how washing and light affect colour) and assists in achieving strong and clear shades that last. Once you become more confident in your dyeing skills mordants can also be used to influence or change the colour palette of a dye, but you don't need to think about this until you have some experience with the process.

I often stress that scouring is the foundation of successful dyeing but the importance of mordanting cannot be overlooked. When novice dyers have weak or blotchy colours, or colours that wash out, it can often be traced back to skipping or rushing through these initial steps. I know how exciting it can be to want to put your fibre in the dye pot but if you can take your time and prepare your fibres thoroughly you will be much happier with your results.

Not only are there a variety of different mordants used in natural dyeing, there are different ways to mordant. Experienced dyers will have their own method and because of this the information out there can be conflicting or confusing. That being the case just know that there are many ways to get to the same or similar place. Before we get into which mordants to use, let me explain a little about the different kinds of mordants commonly used.

Mordants can be sourced from mineral or plant sources.

Mineral-based Mordants

Mineral-based mordants are derived from naturally occurring or synthetically produced minerals. These minerals come in the form of metallic salts such as aluminium, iron, copper, chrome and tin. Chrome, copper and tin are heavy metals and because of their toxic nature I would avoid the use of these for health and environmental reasons. Personally, I use alum (potassium aluminium sulphate) and iron as mordants and as a way to shift (change or modify) colours. Iron is a heavy metal but can be used safely in small quantities.

Plant-based Mordants

Plant-based mordants are sourced from natural substances high in 'tannin' and although they are not technically a mordant in the same way as a metallic salt, they can be used as a more natural alternative to mineral-based mordants. Certain leaves, nuts, seeds and bark contain high levels of tannic acid and this can be used as a natural and safe mordant. Tannins can be clear or they can impart a warm base colour to the fibre you are dyeing. Keep this in mind if you are looking for truer colours as the tannin may influence the resulting shade. The most common tannin used is oak gall, but acorn, walnut, chestnut, myrobalan, *Symplocos*, rhubarb leaves and staghorn sumac are also popular with some dyers.

Mordants Can Influence Colour

Not only do mordants fix and increase longevity, they can also influence the range of colours possible from a dye. Some dyers choose mordants based on the effect they will have on the colour of the dye and others choose based on personal preference. For example, iron will 'sadden' or dull colours, aluminium will brighten colours, and a golden-based tannin will add a warm tone to the dye. If you were to mordant three pieces of fibre in three different types of mordant, you would get three different shades from the same dye. This can be a wonderful discovery when expanding the range of colours possible from one dye.

When Do I Mordant?

Mordanting can be done in a few ways: prior to dyeing, which is known as premordanting; along with the dye in the pot (called one-pot dyeing); or after dyeing, known as post-mordant. There is no right or wrong choice; however, I recommend premordanting as this way you will have more control over the final colour.

Which Mordant Do I Use?

The general rule of thumb is: plant fibres, such as linen, cotton or hemp, can be mordanted with a natural tannin mordant. A simple tannin to use on these types of fibres is oak gall, sometimes sold as tannin powder, but any plant-based mordant will suffice.

For animal fibres, such as wool or silk, I use potassium aluminium sulphate or alum. When used in correct quantities, alum is non-toxic, safe to handle and can be disposed of safely. You should always dispose of your dyes and mordants responsibly (see page 26).

How Much Mordant Do I Use?

In natural dying you will see WOF meaning weight of fibre. This is based on the weight of the fibre to be dyed once it has been scoured and dried. The amount of mordant you use is based on the weight of your fibre, so make sure you weigh your fibre and write the weight down. This is where weighing scales come in handy.

PLANT FIBRES:

100 g (3½ oz) of fibre : 1 teaspoon oak gall or similar tannin
For example, if you have a piece of clothing that weighs 150 g (5 oz) you would use 1½ teaspoons tannin

ANIMAL FIBRES:

100 g (3½ oz) fibre : 2 teaspoons alum
For example, if your fibre weighs 250 g (9 oz) you would use 5 teaspoons alum

---

How to Mordant Plant Fibre

1. Weigh the fibre to be mordanted and calculate the amount of tannin to use. Soak your fibre in a container of water for at least 1–2 hours prior to mordanting.

2. Fill a large container with water (18 l per 500 g [1 lb 2 oz] fibre). Measure your tannin and dissolve in 250 ml (8 fl oz) warm water, whisking until completely dissolved.

3. Add the tannin mixture to the large container of water and stir.

4. Add your scoured, pre-soaked fibre and soak for 08 hours or overnight, stirring frequently. Remove and rinse. If moving onto dyeing, leave the fibre to soak in water.

How to Mordant Animal Fibre

1. Weigh the fibre to be mordanted. Soak your fibre in a container of water for at least 4 hours before mordanting.

2. Fill a container with water (18 l per 500 g [1 lb 2 oz] fibre). Measure your alum, dissolve in a bowl of warm water and add to the large container of water. Stir.

3. Squeeze out your fibre and add this to the mordant solution for at least 12 hours, stirring frequently.

4. Remove your fibre and rinse. If moving onto dyeing leave the fibre to soak in water until you are ready to dye.

Storing Mordants

If you are planning to dye straightaway you can soak your scoured and mordanted fibre in a container of water while you prepare your dye bath. If you don't think you will have time to dye immediately, then dry your items fully and store your fibre until you are ready. Once your items are mordanted they will stay mordanted and you will not have to repeat this step.

Mordants can be stored and used as a base for your next mordanting session. Keep in clearly labelled airtight jars in a cool, dry place out of reach of children and pets. Depending on what time of year it is, I store mordants for 2–4 weeks. However, if you live in a warmer climate, then you may notice your mordant going mouldy sooner.

Disposing of Mordants

Alum, iron and tannin in small quantities can be diluted and disposed of in the garden or down the drain. If you have a garden I would recommend diluting the mordant and pouring it onto the soil of acid-loving plants, such as acer, heather, hydrangea, azaleas or magnolia.

To be extra safe with alum or iron mordant, add 1 teaspoon washing soda, soda crystals or sodium bicarbonate to neutralise the liquid, then you can safely dispose of it down the drain or in your garden.

Always keep away from children and pets.

Mordanting With Soy

Soy is one of the most environmentally destructive crops to cultivate. It requires vast amounts of water and, as demand increases, tragic acres of the rainforest are decimated to make room for this plant. I don't understand the point of mordanting with soy when other less destructive, plant-based mordants work so well. The purpose of mordanting with this plant is to change a plant/cellulose fibre to respond like an animal or protein fibre, as animal fibres are known for taking colour more intensely. I have had a lot of success achieving deep, rich hues on plant-based fibres and especially so with linen.

A Quick Note on Mordanting

I know when you are first starting out this can be a lot to take in and digest, and it can feel a little overwhelming trying to figure everything out and remember what to do. Take it in small steps, first scour, then mordant, then dye. With a little practise, these steps will become more familiar and before long you will be creating beautiful, longlasting, natural colours.

Dye Types

Some dyes are high in tannic acid, which helps the dye bond to the fibre without the addition of a mineral salt mordant. It is only through experience that you will begin to know the types of dyes you are working with and whether you need the addition of a mordant or not. There are four different types of dye.

Substantive Dyes

These dyes have high levels of tannic acid which bind the dye to the fibre, fixing the dye without the addition of a mordant. These dyes often come from the nuts, seeds, heartwood or barks of trees.

Adjective Dyes

There are many dyes that fall into this category. They need the help of a mordant to fix the dye to the fibre. Many of these dyes can be found in the garden and outdoors, such as flowers or leaves.

Fugitive Dyes

As the name suggests, these make a run for it and don't have good fixing properties, even with the addition of a mordant. They are not colour-fast and will fade quickly if exposed to light or washing. Examples of these dyes are beetroot, turmeric and blackberries.

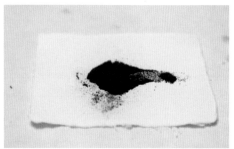

Vat Dyes

These dyes are different to all the other types of dye and need a specific environment to make the dye molecules soluble in water. Examples of vat dyes are indigo and woad. You don't need a mordant when dyeing with indigo as it bonds to the fibre under the right conditions.

THE DYEING PROCESS

UNDERSTAND YOUR FIBRE

It is important to understand the fibre you are working with so you can get good results from your efforts. Each fibre is treated differently in how they are scoured, mordanted and dyed.

See pages 15–16

PREPARE YOUR FIBRE

To prepare your fibre it needs to be cleaned thoroughly to remove any chemicals, oils or waxes so the natural dye can be absorbed as fully as possible. This process is called scouring.

See pages 18–21

MORDANT YOUR FIBRE

After scouring, your fibre needs one more step before dyeing. It needs to be mordanted. A mordant helps to fix the dye to the fibre, increase colour fastness and produce strong and clear colours.

See pages 22–6

FORAGE
& GATHER

There are lots of places to
find ingredients for dyeing.
Look in the kitchen as many
by-products of cooking can
be used to create colour.
Outside, many flowers,
plants and trees make
excellent sources of colour.

*See pages 32–5, pages 36–7,
pages 52–70*

SET UP DYE BATHS
& DYE YOUR FIBRE

Creating your dye bath is
easy. Plant material is added
to a pot of water, which is
gently heated to extract the
dye. The dyestuff is then
removed and the prepared
fibre is added and left until
the desired depth of shade
is achieved.

See pages 36–7, pages 38–9

AFTERCARE

When you are happy with
the colour, remove your
fibre from the dye bath,
rinse with a pH-neutral
soap and hang to dry. Be
sure to wash similar dye
colours together.

*See pages 40–1, page 43,
page 72*

Gathering, Foraging & Collecting Natural Dyes

'And into the forest I go, to lose my mind and find my soul' John Muir

There are many places to find the ingredients for natural dyes. The first and most comfortable place to start is in the centre of your home, the kitchen. From here, the by-products of cooking, ingredients that may be discarded or overlooked, can be used to create the most beautiful range of colours.

The first dye I encourage novice natural dyers to begin with is avocado or onion skins. The stones and skins of avocado give the most beautiful shades of blush, pink and coral. Onion skins, both yellow and red, can slowly accumulate, the yellows giving soft golden hues, the reds soft or rich pinky-browns. You can also dye with black tea, coffee, turmeric, pomegranate, hibiscus flowers, sumac, carrot tops, red cabbage and black beans (see page 52). If you live alone or don't consume much, consider asking friends or your local café to save stones, onion skins or coffee grinds for you. Most cafés are delighted for their waste to be used in such a purposeful way.

Foraging Outside

For those of you who have gardens or access to neighbourhood plants, there is a host of dye sources outside your door. Dyes can be made from many common plants, from all parts of the dandelion and the roots and leaves of dock, to nettles and a variety of flowers such as heather, elderflower, *Coreopsis*, gorse, marigold, dahlia, thyme, rosemary, lavender and the darker flowers of hollyhocks.

If you or anyone you know has rhubarb growing in the garden, apart from being an excellent dessert ingredient, the leaves can be boiled up and used as a plant-based mordant and the roots can be used as a dye. If you do work with rhubarb, please note that the leaves contain oxalic acid which is poisonous and should not be eaten. Although the heat renders the leaves safe to work with, make sure you have proper ventilation when simmering the leaves. (If possible, set up a dye pot outside.)

Trees are an excellent and reliable source of natural colour. Often high in tannin, the bark, leaves, nuts or seeds can be used. In Ireland we have the strong and mighty oak, not to mention pine, hazel, alder, willow, birch, beech and buckthorn. Many species of eucalyptus leaves and bark yield an incredible variety of colour. Those of you fortunate to have fruit trees growing close by can use the leaves or branches as a wonderful source of dye.

Educate Yourself With the Plants Growing Around You

Wherever you are based, it is satisfying to take a walk and forage for colour. Each locality holds the colours of its landscape in its flora and this will be reflected in your dye palette. It is a simple way to connect with your environment and educate yourself about plants growing around you. In doing so you may make many surprising discoveries about what is edible and what can be used as a source of dye. I encourage you to take a walk and look at the trees and plants with a newfound sense of curiosity and wonder.

A Few Points to Keep in Mind When Foraging:

• Always respect the area where you forage.

• Bring a pair of sharp scissors or secateurs and a bag or basket to carry your plants.

• Be careful with stinging nettles or any other plants that may have barbs on the stems or leaves. Wear gloves if needed.

• Only pick that which is in abundance and only take what you need.

• If you can, take what has fallen first. It can be very satisfying to take a walk after a storm when the ground is full of fallen plant material.

• Pick with care so as not to damage the plant, especially if you would like to experiment with tree bark. Take the pieces that have fallen to the ground as stripping a tree of its bark could make it vulnerable to infection.

• Always do your research and know what you are picking; some things are poisonous; others may release noxious gases.

• Don't be a sneaky plant thief. Always ask your neighbours before stealing their plants.

• Don't pick protected species or in protected areas.

• Most importantly, enjoy the process, be curious and have fun learning and experimenting with new plant material. Always remember to be conscious and considerate of your environment.

Storing Plant Material

Depending on your circumstances, it may take a few days to prepare and mordant fibre, gather dye plants and create your dye pots. You can't always use the plants straightaway, or you may need to wait and pick more. If that's the case you may need to store your plants.

To dry plant materials, spread everything out on newspaper or cardboard. Separate the pieces so that nothing overlaps and turn frequently to ensure they dry thoroughly.

Keep an eye on your stored items and check regularly to make sure they don't develop mould.

• Always dry plants fully and never store damp material.

• Don't store items in plastic bags or containers, as mould will develop.

• Store in paper bags, away from direct sunlight, in a cool, dry environment.

• Make sure pieces are well-ventilated and the air can circulate throughout.

• Turn frequently to dry thoroughly and avoid the development of mould.

• Space permitting, keep flowers and seeds in the freezer, otherwise dry and store as described.

• Label everything clearly and keep away from children and pets.

If I am gathering flowers or avocado stones and am not going to use them straightaway, I prefer to store them in the freezer. I find freezing often intensifies the colours yielded from these materials.

Preparing Plants for Dye

When preparing plant materials for your dye bath, most dye material will be in the form of roots, bark, branches, twigs, leaves or flowers. Some plant materials will need to be chopped up to fit in your pot, while others need to be broken up to expose more surface area and extract the dye. Smaller plant material, such as onion skins, flower heads, petals and avocado stones, can go straight in as they are.

When figuring out how much dye stuff to use, the general rule of thumb is equal parts plant material to scoured and dried fibre. To calculate how much dye you need, first weigh your fibre (after it has been scoured), then measure the corresponding amount of dyestuff. For example, if you are dyeing a set of linen napkins and they weigh 100 g (3½ oz), then use 100 g (3½ oz) of plant material. This will give you a good starting point with the colours. If you would like lighter shades you can halve this and for stronger colours you can double. Of course, there will always be exceptions as some dyes will be stronger and more concentrated that others.

Roots, Bark & Branches, Nuts or Seeds

Quantity: 2–3 parts dye material to WOF

Note: If working with roots, remove as much of the earth as possible before cutting.

Roots, tree bark and branches should be broken or chopped into smaller pieces and soaked in cold water for a few days or longer if possible, before extracting the dye. Most tree bark will break or tear easily.

To extract the dye, after soaking, place in a dye pot, cover with boiling water and simmer gently for 1–3 hours. Turn off the heat, leave to cool completely, then strain out all the plant material.

Flowers

Quantity: equal parts flowers to WOF

Can be used in their whole form and do not need to be chopped up.

To extract the dye, place in a dye pot, cover with boiling water and simmer gently for 30 minutes. Turn off the heat, leave to cool completely, then strain out all the plant material.

Leaves

Quantity: 2 parts leaves to WOF

Remove the leaves from the stalk or branches and cut up.

To extract the dye, place in a dye pot, cover with boiling water and simmer gently for 1–2 hours. Turn off the heat, leave to cool completely, then strain out all the leaves.

Creating a Dye Bath

Creating your very first dye bath is a beautiful endeavour. Nothing quite compares to the excitement of getting to this point after carefully scouring and mordanting your fibre, foraging for plants and preparing your plants for dye. There is so much time involved in the preparation that the act of dyeing is often the quickest part of the process.

A dye bath can be compared to brewing a huge pot of tea. Plant material is added to a pot of water and heat is applied to extract the dye. Once extracted, the dyestuff is removed and the fibre is added.

The amount of time needed to extract each dye will differ depending on what dye material you choose. Some things need to simmer for hours to release the colour, other dyes are more immediate. For example, black tea extracts rapidly once hot water is added and is often ready after 15 minutes, whereas avocado stones can take a few hours to release their dye. On occasion, a dye that usually takes 1–2 hours to extract on any given day may take twice as long when you find yourself pushed for time! It is essential to be patient and make sure you have a strong dye bath before adding your fibres to the pot. Do your research on the specific dye you are using and follow the necessary steps. It is only through practise that you will familiarise yourself with the nuances of this process.

In terms of how much water to use, when I first start extracting the dye, I cover it completely with warm or hot water and leave it to stand for about 1 hour before heating on the stove (the longer you can leave it, the better). Once on the stove, I fill my pots three-quarters full of water making sure there is enough room to add, remove or stir the fibre, and always top up the water if necessary. If you prefer to work with specifics, use 1 part plant material to 2 parts water or as a very rough guide you will need about 5 litres water for every 100 g (3½ oz) fibre.

A Few Things to Keep in Mind When Creating a Dye Bath

• The more plant material you use and the longer you leave your fibre in the dye pot, the darker your colours will be.

• For lighter shades, halve the amount of dyestuff used and remove your fibre after 20–30 minutes.

• For darker shades, double the dyestuff and leave the fibre in the dye bath overnight.

• Compared to when it is wet, the dry fibre will appear 2–3 shades lighter. If you want to replicate a colour that you have previously dyed, place a swatch of the dyed cloth in water to see what it looks like wet.

• Always use gentle heat when extracting and dyeing fibre.

• If you find yourself unhappy with the results you can always add more plant material to increase the strength.

Preparing Swatches

I always encourage dyers to test their dyes on small swatches of fibre before committing larger pieces of fibre or garments to the dye pot. To prepare swatches, using scoured, mordanted fibre, cut it into small squares or rectangles, then presoak in a basin of water for 15–20 minutes. Add to the dye pot and leave them in for increments of 10 minutes, 30 minutes, 1–2 hours and overnight.

How to Create a Dye Bath

1. Weigh your scoured, mordanted and dried fibre and make a note of the weight. Presoak your fibre in a container of water while you prepare your dye bath.

2. Weigh your plant material and prepare it accordingly.

3. Fill a pot three-quarters full with water and heat. Add the prepared plant material and bring to a gentle simmer. Simmer until the dye extracts.

4. Turn off the heat and leave your dye bath to cool. Once your dye has cooled, strain out your plant material. The dye is now ready.

Dyeing Methods

As you may be starting to see, there are quite a few ways to do almost every step of this process. The guides on these pages are only guides and not hard and fast rules, except for the part about not adding animal fibres to hot liquid – that's a golden rule! These are the methods that work for me, but they may not work for everyone. I strongly encourage you to experiment and find the way that feels right for you.

Once you have finished preparing your plants and creating your dye bath, there are a few different ways to apply the dye to your fibre.

Cool Dyeing: Animal Fibres

This method is best suited for use on animal fibres; it requires less energy, so if you have limited space or heat sources this may suit you best. I recommend cold dyeing when you first start working, but once you get familiar with the process you can slowly add heat at low temperatures.

To use this method Once the dye material has been simmered and the dye extracted, strain out the plant material. Wait for your dye bath to cool completely, then add your scoured, mordanted and presoaked fibre. Leave your goods in the dye, stirring frequently. When you are happy with the depth of shade, leave for 15–30 minutes, then remove the fibre from the pot. Rinse with a pH-neutral soap and hang to dry. For darker colours, leave your fibre in the dye overnight.

Hot Dyeing: Linen, Cotton, Hemp

The application of heat will reduce the amount of time it takes for the dye to be extracted and absorbed by the fibre. Hot dyeing works incredibly well on plant fibres such as linen, cotton or hemp.

To use this method Once the dye material has been simmered and the dye extracted, strain out the plant material. Add your scoured, mordanted and presoaked plant fibre. Apply heat to the dye bath and simmer for at least 30 minutes, making sure the fibre is moving freely. Stir frequently. When you are happy with the shade, leave for 15–30 minutes, then remove the fibre from the pot. Rinse with a pH-neutral soap and hang to dry. For darker colours, leave the fibre in the pot overnight.

Solar Dyeing: Skeins of Wool

This method works well for testing a small amount of fibre or skeins of wool. It requires heat from the sun to extract the dye. It can be a great way to introduce children to the world of natural dyes or merely a fun project to do together.

To use this method Place your scoured, mordanted and presoaked fibre in a large glass jar, add your dyestuff, fill to the brim and cover with a well-fitting lid. Leave the container in the sunniest spot in your home for at least two days or longer for stronger colours. Once you are happy with the colour remove your pieces from the jar. Rinse with a pH-neutral soap and hang to dry.

Frequently Asked Questions

When it comes to dyeing, there are a few common questions that beginners often have.

When Do I Take My Fibre Out?

Deciding when to take your fibre out is up to you. Colour is such a personal preference and is different for everyone. Remember that when fibre is wet, it will be 2–3 shades darker than when it has been rinsed and dried. Once you see the colour you like, leave it in for another 15–30 minutes before taking it out. For more robust colours, use more dye and leave the fibre in the dye pot for longer.

Can I Reuse My Dye Bath?

Yes, you can reuse your dye bath until it is 'exhausted'. The first pieces you dye in your bath will always be the strongest. On each successive dip after that the dye gets lighter and lighter until the fibres absorb all the colour and there is no dye left. It is beautiful to see the graduating shades from one single dye pot.

Can I Combine Dye Colours?

Yes, you can, and it is a great way to create unique and signature shades. When combining colours, keep the dyes separate. You can, of course, combine both dyes in one pot but I find it is harder to control that way. Dye in your initial colour, remove from the pot, rinse thoroughly, then add to the second dye.

If I Dye Something and Don't Like It, Can I Redye It?

Yes, you can. If you realise you are not happy with it once you have washed and dried it, wash it with 1 teaspoon soda ash or 1 tablespoon soda crystals. Do not add detergent. You can then redye your fibre.

Do I Need to Remordant If I Redye Something?

No, once you mordant something, it is mordanted and you do not need to repeat this step.

How Do I Dispose of My Dye?

You can safely dispose of your dye bath down the drain or in your garden. Rotate where you dispose of your dye. If you have added mineral-based salts to your dye, see page 26 for instructions on how to safely dispose of mordants.

Will My Colours Wash Out?

All things naturally change over time, that is where the beauty lies. They, similar to us, will change through the years. There is something beautiful about a garment or textile that holds history in its fibres. If you have scoured and mordanted thoroughly, your colours should be colourfast, standing up to washing and exposure to light. That said, they will gradually change over time. If you leave dyed pieces directly in the sun, they may fade and bleach, so keep that in mind if you live in a warm and sunny climate. If something fades you can always add it back to the dye pot.

Modifiers

With a little bit of practise, you will soon start to see the most beautiful natural hues emerge from your dye pots. One of the aspects of natural dyeing that makes it so consuming and engaging is the unlimited possibilities of colour available to you.

Once you become familiar with the process and your confidence grows, you may want to start exploring these possibilities by expanding your palette, which is where modifiers come in. Modifiers are something you add to the initial dyeing to change or 'modify' the colour of your fibre, expanding the range of colours available to you.

Modifiers work by shifting the pH of the dye. Some dyes are more sensitive to pH than others, depending on the dye you are working with and the modifier in question. The results can range from subtle to dramatic. There are a few different types of modifiers available to us which come from acidic, alkaline or metallic salts sources.

When you are working with modifiers always test on swatches before modifying large pieces of fibre or garments. Consider keeping notes and add these swatches to your dye journal.

Acidic Modifiers

such as vinegar, lemon juice, lime juice or citric acid
These will shift colours towards reds, warm shades of orange, yellow or pink depending on which dye you use.

Alkaline Modifiers

bicarbonate of soda (baking soda), baking powder, soda crystals and wood or soda ash
These will change dye colours in a variety of different ways. They often shift purples and pinks towards blue or yellows and reds towards pink.

Metallic Salt Modifiers

iron, copper or aluminium
Each metallic salt alters colour differently. Iron tends to dull, sadden or darken colours, aluminium will brighten and copper makes colours greener in tone. If you use these as a modifier, they will also act as a mordant, increasing the colour fastness of your fibre.

How to Use Modifiers

Use 1 teaspoon modifier : 1 l water (except for iron, see pages 46–9 for instructions on using iron as a mordant).

1. Fill a container (large enough for the fibre to move freely) with water. If using a liquid add 1 teaspoon modifier to a small container of water and stir.

2. If using a powder, dissolve 1 teaspoon modifier in 250 ml (8½ fl oz/1 cup) warm water, then add this to your container of water and stir.

3. Remove your fibre from the dye bath, squeeze out excess dye and add it to the modifier. Move your fibre around so the modifier reaches every part of your fibre.

4. Leave the fibre in the modifier, gently moving it around until you get the desired colour change, then remove, rinse in pH-neutral soap and hang to dry.

Iron As a Modifier

One of my favourite mordants to work with is iron. Not only is it excellent at increasing the colour fastness of natural dyes, it is also one of the most dramatic ways to expand your colour range.

Iron is said to sadden or dull colours, but for me there is nothing sad or dull about iron. It is dramatic, intense, adds depth, richness, expansion and possibilities. It can change yellow to green, beige to grey and pinks or reds to rich mauves. As a novice dyer, it is something to add to your natural dyeing process. When I first discovered the character of iron, the excitement of these newfound possibilities was almost too much to contain.

You can make iron water using a homemade method, described on page 48, or by purchasing it in a powder form sold as ferrous sulphate. It can be used before dyeing, added in small quantities to the dye pot or applied after dyeing. How you decide to apply it is up to you. I like to use iron separately after dyeing as I get the most control this way. If you add iron to the dye pot, it will permanently change your dye colour and commit you fully to this darker colour. When applying fibre to an iron bath, you only need to dip and remove quickly to see the results. Some people use heat when working with iron. I use warm water to dissolve the iron powder, but I always use cold water when applying iron to fibre or garments. Heat in combination with iron can be permanently damaging to both plant and animal fibres.

Iron's intense nature makes it incredibly tough on animal fibres. In the process of modifying or mordanting, it weakens the fibre structure. It is therefore better suited to plant fibres. If you leave your goods in iron for long periods, it will damage the fibre, making it brittle and harsh to the touch.

Iron will mark anything naturally dyed that it touches. If you have it on your hands and touch a beautifully dyed piece of fibre, you will leave a permanent mark from contact.

Although iron can be used safely in small quantities, it is a heavy metal and ferrous sulphate is harmful if ingested. Handle it with care and exercise caution when working with iron.

Working With Iron:

• Always wear a mask and gloves.

• Clean tools, work surfaces or anything that comes in contact with iron.

• Have a set of equipment (wooden spoon, container, bowl for mixing, teaspoon for measuring) that you use only with iron; label it clearly and keep it separate to avoid marking other plant-dyed material.

• Do not leave pieces in iron water for extended periods as it can damage fibre – a quick dip is all it needs.

• Wash goods immediately after modifying.

• If you are doing your dyeing in the house, consider labelling and storing your tools away from the kitchen to avoid potential mix-up.

• Make sure to keep iron water out of reach of children and pets.

• Use an eco-friendly fabric conditioner when washing pieces modified with iron. This will counteract the brittle quality that often results from iron.

Iron water can be easily made at home using some rusty nails and vinegar. When you create the iron solution and add it to water it is referred to as an 'iron bath' (see page 48).

Homemade Iron Water

1. Place a handful of rusty nails or rusty metal in a bowl (wire wool works).
2. Add 4 tablespoons white vinegar : 8 tablespoons water.
3. Leave uncovered for at least a week, but longer if possible.
4. Once the solution turns a rusty orange colour, it is ready.
5. Using a muslin cloth, strain this solution into a container.

To Make an Iron Bath

1. Place equal parts water to equal parts iron solution in a container large enough to dye pieces.
2. Add the dyed, rinsed and presoaked goods to the iron water.
3. Leave for 1 minute for a gentle change in colour, longer for more robust results.
4. Remove and wash immediately with a pH-neutral soap and an eco-friendly fabric conditioner.

Iron Water Using Ferrous Sulphate

1. Fill a container with 2.5 l water.

2. In a separate container, dissolve ¼ teaspoon iron in 60 ml (2 fl oz/¼ cup) warm water and stir until dissolved.

3. Use a muslin cloth to strain this solution into the larger container of water and stir.

4. Add your previously dyed, rinsed and presoaked goods to the iron water, 1 minute for a gentle change in colour, longer for a more dramatic change.

5. Remove and wash immediately with a pH-neutral soap and an eco-friendly fabric conditioner.

When Experimenting With Iron

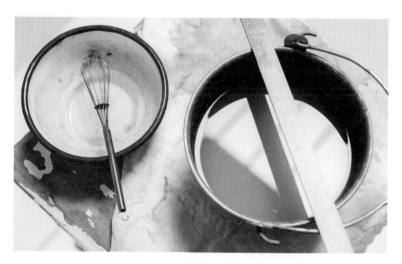

Remember to always test your swatches before committing to larger pieces. Make sure to wash and dry your swatches entirely before adding to your dye journal. If you put wet swatches from an iron bath next to previously dyed swatches, the iron will impact everything it touches.

FIBRE & DYE

avocado on cotton

hibiscus on linen

avocado on wool

hibiscus on cotton

avocado + iron on silk

hibiscus + iron on linen

hibiscus + iron on silk

avocado on silk

hibiscus on silk

nettles + iron on silk

black tea + iron on silk

hibiscus on wool

nettles on silk

nettles + iron on linen

avocado + iron on linen

alder cones + iron on silk

black tea + iron on linen

yellow onion skins
on linen

olive leaves on wool

yellow onion skins on linen

yellow onion skins on cotton

yellow onion skins
on cotton

olive leaves + iron on silk

olive leaves on silk

black tea on silk

black tea on cotton

yellow onion skins on silk

olive leaves + iron on linen

alder cones on silk

black tea on linen

yellow onion skins + iron
on silk

yellow onion skins +
iron on linen

black tea on wool

alder cones on cotton

Dyeing With Food Waste

Now that we have covered the basics of natural dyeing, it is time to start putting it into practise. We will begin with everyday dyes you can access in your kitchen through ingredients or food waste. If some of these ingredients are not common in your kitchen many of them can be bought inexpensively at your local shop or market.

Then we will move outside and dye with materials you can find in your garden, neighbourhood, parks or surrounding countryside. When choosing where to start with natural dyes, you can begin by thinking about what colours appeal to you most and work backwards, or you can look at what grows abundantly all around you.

The wonderful thing about starting with kitchen ingredients is that you don't have to invest in any expensive materials to begin. You can take what may otherwise be deemed as waste and turn it into something beautiful. Start collecting your ingredients, whether it is from a morning cup of tea, coffee or your dinner. Quite a few raw materials, such as avocado stones, onion skins, tea, coffee and pomegranate skins, have high levels of tannic acid naturally present. Tannic acid acts as a natural binder fixing the colour to the fibre, which means you don't need to mordant. If you have yet to buy tannin powder to use as a mordant, you can start straightaway without it.

Once you start accessing colour in this way, your kitchen ingredients and compost bin will take on new meaning and potential. It may take a while for you to collect ingredients for dye, but onion skins, carrot tops, tea and coffee can all be dried and stored in paper bags and avocado stones and skins can be kept in the freezer. Whatever you are collecting, make sure you dry it thoroughly before storing and if you have space in your freezer, consider keeping plant material there (see page 35 on how to store plant material).

What You Can Use in Your Kitchen:

Blues & Purples

red cabbage

black beans

Pinks, Purples & Corals

dried hibiscus flowers – pinks & purples

avocado stones & skin – blush, pink & corals

red onion skins – plums & pinky-browns

Yellows, Orange & Greens

pomegranate skins – yellows

yellow onion skins – yellow & orange

carrot tops – yellow greens to greens

dried camomile flowers – yellows & greens

turmeric – least colourfast but a rich source for yellow, orange, ochre & green (when modified with iron)

Tan & Browns

black tea – tan, brown & rich earthy tones

coffee – tans & browns

Dyeing With Plants

There are so many plants you can extract dye from, too many to include on these pages. Here is a list of some of the more common plants and the colours that each plant produces. Some may grow in your part of the world and others may not, but wherever you live some of these will be available to get you started on the road to natural dyeing.

Red/Pinks

some lichen, madder, brazilwood, safflower, Lady's bedstraw, cochineal, hibiscus, pear bark, elm bark, hawthorn, hollyhock, rowan, safflower

Orange

Coreopsis flowers, cutch, annatto, eucalyptus leaves, rhubarb roots, madder roots, willow

Yellow/Gold

weld, St John's wort, camomile, fustic, goldenrod, buckthorn berries, gorse flowers, marigold, heather, safflower, *Coreopsis* flowers, yellow cosmos, hawthorn, dahlia flowers, daffodil flowers, sumac leaves, dock leaves, tansy flowers, dandelion flowers & leaves, eucalyptus leaves

Brown

acorn, walnut husks, tea leaves, coffee, alder, cutch, oak gall, eucalyptus bark

Green

yarrow tops, alder, birch, dyer's camomile with iron, rosemary, olive with iron, St John's wort, fustic, goldenrod with iron, weld, rhubarb root, saffron, marigold with iron, heather with iron, safflower, *Coreopsis* with iron, hawthorn, dahlia leaves & stems, ivy leaves, dock leaves with iron, comfrey, tansy flowers & plant tops, nettles

Blue

indigo, woad, blackberries with iron, elderberries with iron

Violet

logwood, dyer's alkanet, hibiscus flowers, dark flowers of hollyhock, elderberries, blackthorn fruits, mahonia berries, blackberries

Black

logwood with iron, oak gall with iron, walnut with iron

Dyeing With Onion Skins

Allium cepa

A common ingredient in everyday cooking, the onion, both red and yellow, can be used to create a warm range of golden colours. Similar to black tea, it is high in tannin making mordanting optional. It is inexpensive to purchase, easy to collect and surprisingly quick to extract the dye.

You can choose to dye with one colour or combine both for deeper, richer shades.

---

dye colour: Yellow skins: yellows, orange, rusts;
Greens when mordanted with iron;
Red skins: plums and pinky-browns;
Deep browns when mordanted with iron

mordant: mordanting is optional, adding it will increase the colour fastness and longevity of the colours achieved
For plant fibres use 1 teaspoon tannin : 100 g (3½ oz) fibre
For animal fibres use 2 teaspoons alum : 100 g (3½ oz) fibre

amount: 100 g (3½ oz) fibre : 5 litre pot
Half the weight of fibre to onion skins; for more robust colours, use equal parts skins to WOF
For example, for 100 g (3½ oz) fibre use 50 g (2 oz) skins

PREPARATION

Onion skins are very easy to work with. All you need to do is place them in the dye pot, cover with water and add heat. There is no need to change them in any way. When collecting enough skins to dye with, make sure you use the dry outer layer, the inside layers can develop mould and get stinky if left as they are. Store them in a brown paper bag out of direct sunlight.

MAKING A DYE BATH

1. Add your skins to the dye pot and cover with water.

2. Place on the stove and bring to a simmer.

3. Simmer gently for 30–45 minutes. Once the colour of the water has changed and deepened in strength, the dye is extracted. This can take anywhere from 30 minutes–1 hour.

4. Take off the heat and leave to cool completely, then use a sieve to strain out the skins.

5. Your dye is now ready to be used.

Note: If you are dyeing plant material, you can add your scoured, mordanted and presoaked fibre to the dye pot. If you are dyeing animal fibre, you will need to let the dye cool thoroughly before adding your goods.

Opposite l–r & top–bottom: onion skins on linen (45 mins); cotton (1 hr); silk (30 mins); silk (1 hr); cotton velvet (30 mins); silk (2 hrs) + iron after bath; linen (30 mins).

Dyeing With Black Tea

Camellia sinensis

I cannot remember when I had my first cup of tea, but I do remember vividly being taught how to brew tea correctly. Tea is a way for us to connect, to catch up and slow down. It can be a temporary salve or the perfect excuse to eat biscuits and cake (not that anyone ever needs an excuse to eat cake!).

As a dye, tea is one of the most straightforward and underappreciated sources of colour. Not only is it rich in tannin, making mordanting with this plant optional, but it also adds a beautiful rich base when combined with other dyes. It adds depth, softness and warmth to your palette.

---

dye colour: tan, beige, brown, rich golden orange with alum
Light grey to dark graphite when mordanted with iron
If you are looking for greys, the darker you dye it, the darker your grey once mordanted with iron

mordant: mordanting is optional, adding it will increase the colour fastness and longevity of the colours achieved
For plant fibres use 1 teaspoon tannin : 100 g (3½ oz) fibre
For animal fibres use 2 teaspoons alum : 100 g (3½ oz) fibre

amount: 100 g (3½ oz) fibre : 5 litre pot
Equal parts weight of fibre to weight of black tea; for stronger colours use twice the amount of tea to WOF
For example, for 100 g (3½ oz) fibre use 100 g (3½ oz) black tea

PREPARATION

You can use tea bags or leaves, fresh or used. There are many different kinds of black tea. Some will produce browns, some richer orange tones. Keep in mind that unless the bags are sold as biodegradable do not compost them once you are finished. Most tea bags contain plastic microfibres that don't break down. When gathering enough to dye with, make sure they are thoroughly dry before storing. Whatever you are using, it can go straight into the pot and doesn't need any prep.

MAKING A DYE BATH

1. Add your tea to the dye pot, cover with boiling water and leave to stand for 5 minutes.

2. Fill the remainder of the pot three-quarters full with water and place on a heat source.

3. Bring to a gentle boil, then reduce the heat to a simmer and simmer for 30 minutes.

4. Take off the heat and leave to cool completely, then use a sieve to strain out the tea.

5. Your dye is now ready to be used with whichever method is suited to your fibre (see dyeing methods pages 40–1).

Note: If you are dyeing plant material, you can add your scoured, mordanted and presoaked fibre to the pot. If you are dyeing animal fibre, you will need to let the dye cool thoroughly before adding your goods.

Opposite l–r & top–bottom: black tea on linen (30 mins); linen (30 mins) + iron after bath; cotton (30 mins); cotton (30 mins) + iron after bath; linen (1 hr); linen (1 hr) + iron after bath.

56

Dyeing With Avocado Stones

Persea americana

When I first learnt that you could dye with both the stones and skins, I was intrigued. I had no idea they held such a beautiful array of hues. When I dyed with avocado for the first time, I was struck by the distinctness of its aroma as it simmered away and the soft, beautiful femininity of its resulting shades.

You can use the stones, skins or a combination of both.

---

dye colour: depending on where your avocados come from, the variety and the time of year, you can achieve variations of soft blush, pink, coral
With acidic modifiers, you can shift the pinks towards orange
Iron changes the colours towards pinky-greys and mauves

mordant: mordanting is optional, adding it will increase the colour fastness and longevity of the colours achieved
For plant fibres use 1 teaspoon tannin : 100 g (3½ oz) fibre
For animal fibres use 2 teaspoons alum : 100 g (3½ oz) fibre

amount: 100 g (3½ oz) fibre : 5 litre pot
Twice the weight of fibre to avocado
For example, for 100 g (3½ oz) fibre use 200 g (7 oz) avocado

PREPARATION

If you are using the stones, peel the fleshy film from the outside. If using the skins, be sure to clean all the remaining flesh from the inside. Depending on how long it takes you to gather enough to dye with, I recommend storing in an airtight container in the freezer if you have space. If you are quick to consume these, you may want to consider keeping them in a jar of water, refreshing the water as needed. If neither of those appeal to you, make sure to dry thoroughly before storing in brown paper bags. Both the skins and stones can go straight into the pot as they are and do not need any cutting or chopping.

MAKING A DYE BATH

1. Add your avocado stones or skins to the dye pot.

2. Fill three-quarters full with water.

3. Place on the stove and bring to a simmer.

4. Simmer for 1–2 hours until there is a noticeable change in the colour of the liquid.

5. Take off the heat and leave to cool completely, then use a sieve to strain the liquid, removing all parts of the avocado.

6. Your dye is now ready to be used.

Note: Sometimes beginners try dyeing with avocado for the first time only to get murky, brownish results. To avoid this, don't boil the avocado for too long.

Opposite l–r & top–bottom: avocado stone on silk (1 hr); linen (1 hr); wool (2 hrs); linen (1 hr) + iron after bath; cotton (1 hr); linen (30 mins).

Top left: Eucalyptus bark; top right: Eucalyptus swatches; bottom left: Dock leaf swatches; bottom right: Dock leaves.

Dyeing With Trees

Trees

After experimenting with food waste, you may want to start looking at what trees are growing in your area. Leaves, bark, twigs and nuts can often be used a source of natural colour. Some of the more common trees that are used for dye are olive, eucalyptus, oak, alder, willow, walnut and elm. With many fruit trees such as fig, peach, plum, cherry, apricot and apple producing a variety of beautiful shades.

When gathering from trees, remember to take what has fallen first, especially when it comes to the bark.

Leaves of Trees

Use 2 parts leaves : 1 part fibre

Use a pair of sharp scissors to cut the leaves up as much as possible to expose the maximum amount of surface area. Add your leaves to the dye pot and cover with boiling water. Soak for 1–3 days. When you are ready to add heat, fill the pot with water, so it is three-quarters full, and bring to the boil. Reduce the heat and simmer gently for 1–2 hours. Turn off the heat, leave to cool completely, then strain out the leaves.

Bark or Nuts

Use 2–3 parts : 1 part fibre

You can leave nuts whole or chop in half. Break or tear bark into small pieces. Add to the dye pot and cover with boiling water. Soak for 1–3 days. When you are ready to add heat, fill the pot with water, so it is three-quarters full and bring to the boil. Reduce the heat and simmer for 1–3 hours. Turn off the heat, cool, then strain out the plant material.

Dyeing With Nettles

Urtica dioica

Nettles grow abundantly here in Ireland. Most untamed and wild areas, of which there are many, are laden with these perennials. An incredibly versatile plant, its fibrous stems have long been used to make cloth. High in iron and vitamin C, its leaves have been a source of nourishment through soups and teas.

Although its leaves are covered in fine stinging hairs, this plant produces beautiful earthy hues in the dye pot. Nettles will yield different tones depending on the time of year you harvest them.

---

dye colour: khakis, yellows, greens
Darker greens with alum and iron as a modifier

mordant: mordanting is necessary with this plant
For plant fibres use 1 teaspoon tannin : 100 g (3½ oz) fibre
For animal fibres use 2 teaspoons alum : 100 g (3½ oz) fibre

amount: 100 g (3½ oz) fibre : 5 l pot
Twice the weight of fibre in nettles
For example, for 100 g (3½ oz) fibre use 200 g (7 oz) nettles

PREPARATION

Using a pair of sharp scissors, cut off the top few centimetres of the plant into your basket. Nettles can be added straight to the pot as they are. If you are storing, spread them out to dry thoroughly before putting away. Be sure to wear gloves and cover your arms when collecting nettles. Remember if you do get stung, the leaves of the dock leaves, which often grow alongside stinging nettles, have long been used to bring relief.

MAKING A DYE BATH

1. Add your leaves to the dye pot.

2. Cover with boiling water and leave overnight.

3. Top up the water levels in the pot so it is three-quarters full.

4. Place on the stove and bring to a simmer.

5. Simmer for 30 minutes–1 hour.

6. Once the dye is extracted, take off the heat, leave to cool completely, then use a sieve to strain out all the leaves.

7. Your dye is now ready to be used.

Opposite l–r & top–bottom: nettle on silk (1 hr); silk (1 hr) + iron after bath; silk (overnight) + iron after bath; cotton (1 hr); Merino wool (1 hr); linen (2 hrs).

Dyeing With Olive Leaves

Olea europaea

Although traditionally associated with a beautifully warm Mediterranean climate, there are a surprising amount of olive trees growing in Irish gardens. Although the olive tree is hardy enough to survive an Irish winter, unfortunately there is not enough sun for them to produce olives.

As a dye source, the leaves of this tree produce the brightest, most beautiful clear yellows.

---

dye colour: bright clear yellow to sage
Dark green with an iron mordant

mordant: mordanting is necessary
For plant fibres use 1 teaspoon tannin : 100 g (3½ oz) fibre
For animal fibres use 2 teaspoons alum : 100 g (3½ oz) fibre

amount: Use 2 parts leaves : 1 part fibre
For example, for 100 g (3½ oz) fibre use 200 g (7 oz) leaves

PREPARATION

Remove the leaves from the stalk or branches. Use a pair of sharp scissors to cut the leaves up as much as possible to expose the maximum amount of surface area.

MAKING A DYE BATH

1. Cut up your leaves and place in the dye pot.

2. Cover with boiling water and simmer gently for 1–2 hours, then turn off the heat and leave to soak for 1–3 days.

3. When ready to extract the dye, top up the water levels in the pot so it is three-quarters full.

4. Place on the stove and bring to a simmer.

5. Simmer gently for 1–2 hours.

6. Once the dye is extracted, take off the heat, leave to cool completely, then use a sieve to strain out all the leaves.

7. Your dye is now ready to be used.

Opposite l–r & top–bottom: olive leaf on cotton (1 hr); silk (2 hrs); silk (2 hrs) + iron after bath; linen (1 hr); Merino wool (2 hrs).

How Do I Get Green Naturally?

Although green is seen abundantly in nature, it can be a little challenging getting true rich greens straight from the dye pot. Plant dyes are full of surprises and this was one of those colours that took me a while to understand.

There are some plants that give you tones and shades of green direct from the dye pot such as nettle, but their tones are subtle and the colours can change with the seasons. To get a true green naturally you have to modify a yellow with either iron or copper. The other option is to layer a blue dye (such as indigo or woad) with a yellow dye (such as weld or fustic). When getting green by modifying or combining, the shade of yellow will determine the shade of green. For example, if you have a bright yellow, this is likely to give you a lime or grass green, whereas orange yellows or mustard yellows will give you richer dark mossy greens. The stronger your yellow, the deeper the shade of green achievable.

PLANTS THAT GIVE GREEN

ivy

comfrey

sunflower

nettle (depending on time of year)

Opposite) l–r & top–bottom: yellow dye (fustic) + blue dye (indigo); yellow onion skins modified with iron water; yellow dye (olive) modified with iron water; bright yellow (olive) + blue dye (indigo); bright yellow (weld) + blue dye (indigo).

MODIFYING YELLOW WITH IRON

There are some dyes that when modified with iron give beautiful shades of green. These are:

weld   *turmeric*

fustic   *goldenrod*

olive leaf   *camomile*

yellow onion skins

When experimenting with greens by modifying a yellow, follow the sequence of scouring, mordanting and dyeing your fibre. When you have finished dyeing, rinse your fabric fully and follow the instructions on pages 48–9 to modify the colour with iron. The longer you leave your fibre in the iron water the darker the change in colour, but remember the precautions and don't leave it in the iron for longer than 5–10 minutes. Once you remove your fibre from the iron rinse thoroughly and then wash with a pH-neutral soap.

COMBINING YELLOW & BLUE

Another way to get green is to dye with a blue, rinse and then 'overdye' with a yellow. Overdyeing is when you dye with one dye, rinse and then dye with another on top of the first dye. Of course, you could do this by dyeing with yellow first and then overdyeing with blue. The best blue dyes to work with are woad and indigo. Both woad and indigo are known as vat dyes (see page 28 for dye types) and require a slightly more complicated process to extract the dye.

Dyeing With Alder Cones

Alnus glutinosa

You are likely to find alder trees along the banks of rivers in parks and damper places. They grow abundantly along the rivers in Dublin and, apparently, they also grow quite well in North America and other parts of Europe. The cones and twigs are very high in tannin and mordanting is not needed when dyeing with these.

However, if dyeing with the leaves, you will need to mordant. Experiment with both and see which one appeals to you most.

---

dye colour: greens, tan, ochres
Darker greens with alum
Greens and dark greys with iron as a modifier

mordant: the cones, twigs and bark are very high in tannin and can be used as an alternative to oak gall powder, because of this mordanting is not necessary

amount: 100 g (3½ oz) fibre : 5 litre pot
2 parts alder : 1 part fibre
For example, for 100 g (3½ oz) fibre use 200 g (7 oz) alder cones

PREPARATION

Plan on gathering alder cones after a storm. The ground will be littered with them. The cones are often attached to the twig and can be added straight to the dye pot. I like to soak my cones for a few days, or longer if possible, before adding heat.

MAKING A DYE BATH

1. Add your cones to the dye pot.

2. Cover with boiling water and leave covered for 1–5 days.

3. Top up the water levels in the pot, so it is three-quarters full.

4. Place on the stove and bring to a simmer.

5. Simmer for 1 hour, or up to 2 hours, depending on the colour you would like to achieve.

6. Once the dye is extracted, take off the heat, leave to cool completely, then use a sieve to strain out all the cones.

7. Your dye is now ready to be used.

Opposite l–r & top–bottom: alder cones on linen (1 hr); wool (1 hr); silk (1 hr); silk (1 hr) + with iron after bath; cotton (1 hr).

Dyeing With Hisbiscus Flowers

Hibiscus

Hibiscus flowers can be a vibrant and deeply satisfying dye to work with. Similar to black tea and onion skins, the flowers release the dye quickly. They don't need any special preparation and can be put straight into the dye pot. If hibiscus doesn't grow locally, it can be found in health food shops and most places that sell spices and dried foods.

I always love ingredients that I can both consume and dye with. Hibiscus falls into that category, making a wonderfully refreshing tea that's loaded with antioxidants!

---

dye colour: pinks, purples, lilac, maroon
Deep mauve with an iron mordant

mordant: for plant fibres use 1 teaspoon tannin : 100 g (3½ oz) fibre
For animal fibres use 2 teaspoons alum : 100 g (3½ oz) fibre

amount: 100 g (3½ oz) fibre : 5 litre pot
Equal parts flowers to WOF
For example, for 100 g (3½ oz) fibre use 100 g (3½ oz) hibiscus

PREPARATION

Store fresh flowers in the freezer until you have gathered enough. If freezing isn't an option, spread your flowers out on newspaper, turning frequently to dry thoroughly. Once dry, store in paper bags or glass containers out of direct sunlight. After use, the flowers can be added to your compost or disposed of in your garden.

MAKING A DYE BATH

1. Add your flowers to the dye pot.

2. Cover with boiling water and leave covered for 1 hour.

3. Top up the water levels in the pot so it is three-quarters full.

4. Place on the stove and bring to a simmer.

5. Simmer for 30 minutes.

6. Once the dye is extracted, take off the heat and leave to cool completely, then use a sieve to strain out all the flowers.

7. Your dye is now ready to be used.

Note: To get the darkest shades from hibiscus flowers, leave your fibres in the dye pot overnight.

Opposite l–r & top–bottom: hibiscus on linen (overnight) + iron after bath; linen (overnight); silk (30 mins); linen (30 mins) + bicarbonate of soda (baking soda) solution; linen (1 hr); cotton (1 hr) + iron after bath.

Keeping a Dye Journal

There are many ways to approach natural dyeing. Some of you might like to experiment freely without ever taking notes and others may like to record every single detail of your process. There is no right or wrong way.

When I first started out I wrote everything down so I could recreate exact colours if I needed to at a later point. The more experience I have with this, the less I write down, unless I come up against a challenge in trying to replicate or achieve a specific shade. My dye books have become something I value greatly, showing my progress and with memories of colour bound to each page.

When I began I would scribble my notes into my book and staple the swatches onto the pages. Now I keep rough notes as I go, later transcribing them neatly into the pages of my journal once the dyeing is finished and the swatches are dry. If you do decide to keep a dye journal, I recommend approaching it almost as a meditative practice, setting time aside to record the fibre type you are using, the dye, the time of year, if you have mordanted it, what you mordanted it with, how much dye you used, how long you keep it in the pot for and any other special considerations.

If keeping notes is not for you then relish the freedom of dyeing without trying to hold on to the results of your experiments. The fibre you dye will be your living journal.

Troubleshooting

These are a few of the most common issues that arise for novice dyers.

Inconsistent or Blotchy Results

May result from:

• Lack of thorough scouring and/or incorrect mordanting (check pages 18–21 and pages 22–6 for instructions on scouring and mordanting). Remember to take your time and do these two steps thoroughly.

• Too much fibre in the dye pot. If your dye pot is too small for the amount of fibre you have in there, try adding less fibre. Remember you want the fibre to be able to move freely to absorb as much of the dye as possible.

• Lack of frequent stirring. Remember to stir your fibres every 15–20 minutes if possible. If you leave them without stirring, the dye particles may settle in an uneven manner and result in inconsistent colour.

Weak Colour

If your colours are coming out weaker than you would like, try adding more plant material to your dye bath. Consider doubling the quantities, simmering for a few hours or leaving your plant material in overnight, either before or after simmering. Don't forget to stir.

Linen Changes Colour in Wash

• The detergent you are using may have chemicals or additives that affect the pH of your plant dyes. Remember to source a pH-neutral soap that won't affect the colour of your plant dyes. Pure Castile liquid soap is a great pH-neutral soap to use, as it is gentle on fibres and won't change or alter the colour of your natural dyes.

• The mineral content of your water may affect the colour you get. Consider testing the pH of your water to see what the pH level is. This will inform you on how it may affect or influence your colour.

Brownish Colours

Sometimes when heat is added to a plant dye for too long it can affect the colour and turn the shades murky. If you are getting browns or murky colours from a dye that should be giving you more defined colour consider simmering at a lower temperature for a shorter amount of time.

Marks When Drying Your Dyed Pieces

If you dry your pieces on a metal radiator, the heat in combination with the dyes and metal may cause strange lines or marks to appear on your fabric. I always recommend hanging your goods up to dry. You want the air to circulate as much as possible and when they are lying flat, they are more likely to come in to contact with elements that may mark or alter the nature of the colour.

DYE-BASED PROJECTS

RENEW WHAT YOU HAVE

The most straightforward place to start with natural dyeing is to dye something you already own. Maybe you have a well-loved T-shirt, a sentimental item of clothing or something that if it was just a different colour would see much more use? If you have kids in your life, maybe you have some items of theirs that could do with a refresh. If you have some old pillowcases, tea towels or napkins, they are always a great place to start. Take a while to think about what you have lying around that could be repurposed through the dye pot.

YOU WILL NEED

One item of clothing; it can be either plant or animal based. I am dyeing an old cotton nightshirt, so the instructions here are for dyeing cotton. For instructions on how to dye animal fibres see page 40.

fabric: 100% cotton

dye material: avocado stones
I have used avocado stones for this project, but feel free to use skins or a combination of both

how much to use: 2 parts avocado : 1 part fibre
This will give you rich shades of pink; for softer colours use equal parts avocado to the weight of fibre. My garment weighs 125 g (4 oz) so I used 250 g (9 oz) stones that were scrubbed and stored in water before dyeing

mordant: mordanting is optional and can be added to increase colour fastness, but it is not required
For plant fibres use 1 teaspoon tannin : 100 g (3½ oz) fibre
For animal fibres use 2 teaspoons alum : 100 g (3½ oz) fibre
I premordanted with 1¼ teaspoons tannin powder

equipment:
container for presoaking
dye pot
tea strainer
wooden spoon

TIME: 1½–10 hrs + scouring
& mordanting

This project will require you to scour your item. As mordanting is optional, you can skip this step if you want to jump straight in and get dyeing! I find it helpful to scour and mordant my items ahead of time, so I can focus on creating the dye bath and dyeing my fibres. Your dye pot needs to be large enough for whatever it is you are dyeing to be able to move freely, without being squashed against the sides of the pot. When your item has space to move in the dye, it absorbs the colour in a more even and consistent manner. Keep in mind if you are dyeing an old T-shirt that has stained armpits, the dyeing may not cover the stains. If you have a heavily stained piece, I recommend scouring extra thoroughly. Follow the instructions on page 19 on how to scour plant fibres (stove-top method).

1. Following the instructions on page 18 and page 24 for scouring and mordanting plant fibres, weigh, scour and mordant your piece, then presoak your fibre in a container of water for 1–2 hours while you prepare the dye bath.

2. Add your avocado stones to the dye pot and fill three-quarters full with water. Place on the stove and bring to a simmer.

3. Simmer for 1–2 hours until there is a noticeable change in the colour of the liquid, then turn off the heat and leave to cool completely. Using a tea strainer, strain the liquid, removing all parts of the avocado.

4. The time it takes for the dye to extract may be different for everyone, so don't worry if it is taking longer than expected. Resist the urge to boil the dye as this may make the colour turn brown and lose its pinkness.

5. Squeeze out the excess water from your fibre and slowly add to the dye bath. Use the wooden spoon to submerge your fibres fully, working out any air pockets.

6. Leave on a gentle simmer for 30 minutes–1 hour. When your fibre becomes the colour you like, turn off the heat and cool. Squeeze out the excess dye and remove from the pot. As this is different for everyone, I can't tell you when to remove your fibres, this part is up to you. Rinse your fibre in pH-neutral soap and hang to dry.

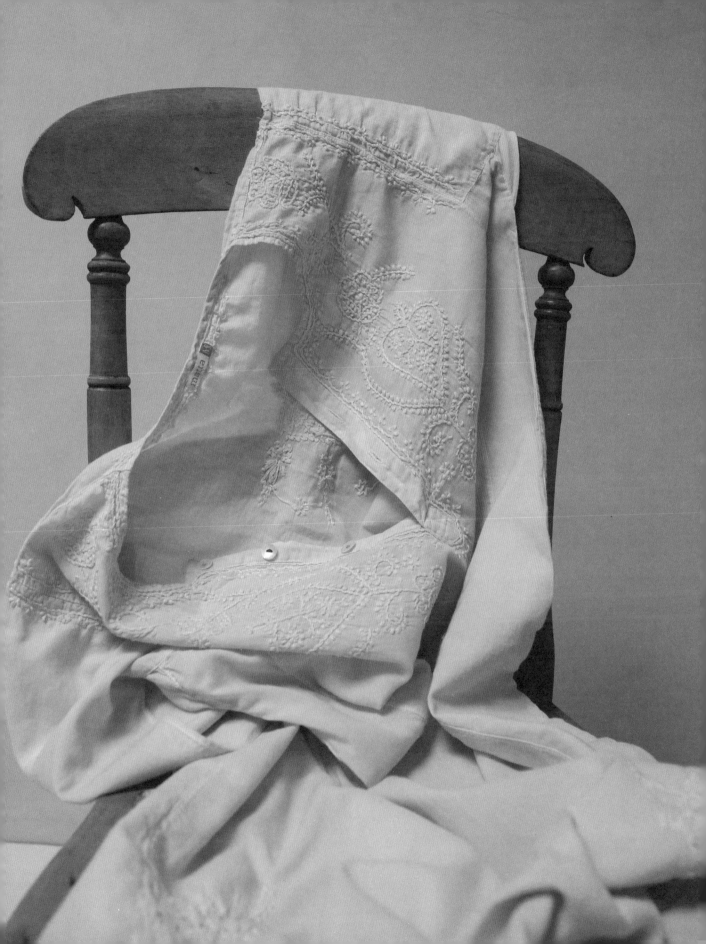

LINEN TABLECLOTH & NAPKINS

There is something beautiful about using food waste to colour the textiles for your table. These instructions make four napkins and one tablecloth, but you can easily make any other variation. I have left the edges torn for a relaxed look and a simple no-sew project. I have used a combination of yellow and red onion skins for a deeper colour, but if you would like a sunnier warm honey tone, then just use yellow skins.

YOU WILL NEED

fabric: linen napkins x 4 (I used midweight linen cut into 4 squares, 42 x 42 cm [17 x 17 in])
I large piece of fabric to fit your table (I used 2 m [2¼ yd])

dye material: onion skins
I used a combination of yellow and red, but feel free to use whichever you use most in your cooking

how much to use: I part onion skins : 2 parts fibre
My tablecloth and napkins had a combined weight of 600 g (1 lb 5 oz). I used 300 g (10½ oz) skins (one-third of which were red). For richer colours, use equal parts skins to WOF

mordant: mordanting will increase colour fastness, but it is not required. I did not mordant these pieces. If you would like to mordant, then follow the instructions on page 24 for mordanting plant fibres using I teaspoon tannin : 100 g (3½ oz) fibre

equipment:
measuring tape
scissors
container for presoaking
dye pot large enough to hold your tablecloth
sieve
wooden spoon

TIME: 1–9 hrs + scouring

This is one of the quicker projects to do if you are pressed for time. You could easily scour, dye and dry your items in one day. If you plan on mordanting, consider doing the scouring and mordanting a day before your dyeing. The onion skins are quick to release their colour and the linen is quick to absorb the dye.

1. For the napkins, cut four pieces of linen large enough to cover your lap. For your tablecloth, measure your table and calculate the size needed, so your linen drapes generously over the sides.

2. Scour your linen following the instructions for scouring plant fibres on page 18 and leave to dry. When the linen is dry, weigh the linen and note the weight, then weigh half the amount in onion skins.

3. Place the linen in a container of water to presoak for at least 1–2 hours while you prepare the dye bath.

4. Add the skins to the dye pot and cover with water. Place on the stove and bring to a simmer. Simmer gently for 30–45 minutes.

5. Once the colour of the water has changed and deepened, the dye is extracted. This can take from 30 minutes–1 hour. Turn off the heat, leave to cool completely, then strain out all the skins.

6. Squeeze out the excess water from your linen and add it to the dye pot. You may need to do this in two stages depending on the size of the pot. Remember not to squash your material into the pot, you always want it to move freely.

7. Return to the heat and simmer gently for 30 minutes, stirring frequently. Turn off the heat and leave the dye bath to cool.

8. When you are happy with the colour, squeeze out the excess dye and remove your fibre from the pot. Leave overnight for stronger colours. Rinse your fibre with pH-neutral soap and hang to dry.

FUROSHIKI-INSPIRED BAG

The Japanese art of furoshiki refers both to a traditional type of cloth and the method used to wrap and transport everyday items and goods with it. This furoshiki-inspired bag is a practical way to store and transport goods. When my girls were younger, these bags were great for holding their lunches. The pattern is based on a rectangle where the length is three times the width. I used linen to make these, but you can make them with any fabric and in any size you like.

YOU WILL NEED

fabric: 100% linen (you can use any plant-based fibre you like)
This project is based on a medium-sized bag measuring 20 × 61 cm (8 × 24 in)

dye material: nettle tops

how much to use: 2 parts nettle : 1 part fibre
My linen weighed 50 g (2 oz), so I used 100 g (3½ oz) nettles

mordant: for plant fibres use 1 teaspoon tannin : 100 g (3½ oz) fibre
As my linen weighed 50 g (2 oz), I used ½ teaspoon tannin

equipment:
measuring tape
scissors and pins
needle and thread
dye pot
sieve
wooden spoon
container for presoaking

TIME: 2–9 hrs + scouring & mordanting

This bag is constructed through a series of three folds. It is relatively straightforward but may seem a little complicated the first time. I recommend mocking this up with a rectangular piece of paper before cutting or sewing the fabric. This will familiarise you with the folds and construction of the bag. Try scouring, mordanting and soaking the nettles the day before and then preparing the dye bath while you are sewing your bag.

MAKING YOUR BAG

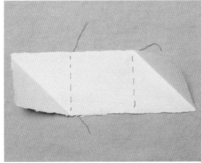

1. Scour and mordant your linen following the instructions on page 18 and page 24 for scouring and mordanting plant fibres. Once it is dry, measure a rectangle where the width is three times the length. Weigh your fibre and note the weight. Lay your linen out flat horizontally.

2. Fold the edge of the left side of the linen in line with the left top edge, then use your fingers to press this in place. Fold the edge of the right side down. The top of the right side should be in line with the edge of the bottom right edge, then use your fingers to press this fold in place.

3. You now have a square in between your two folded sides.

4. Fold the square in half along the diagonal, then use your fingers to press this fold in place.

5. Use a pin to tack in place where both sides of the square meet the folded edge. Sew by hand to secure where the edges touch on both sides. The edges can overlap by 1 cm (½ in) and a simple running stitch should suffice. Your bag is now ready to dye.

6. Measure twice the weight of your linen in nettle leaves.

7. Add the leaves to the dye pot, making sure the pot is large enough for your linen to move freely. Cover with boiling water and leave to soak overnight.

8. Top up the water in the pot, so it is three-quarters full, then place on the stove and bring to a simmer. Simmer for 30 minutes–1 hour until the water changes colour and the dye is extracted.

9. Once the dye is extracted, turn off the heat, leave to cool completely, then strain out all the leaves.

10. Presoak your bag in a container of water for 30–45 minutes until it is soaked through. Squeeze out the excess water, then add the bag to the dye pot.

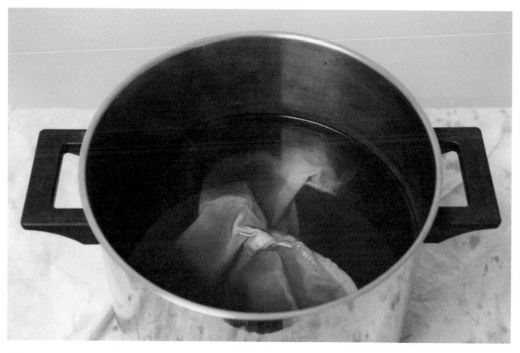

11. Return the dye pot to the heat and simmer gently for 1 hour. Turn off the heat and let your bag sit in the dye until you see the colour you like. Remove from the pot, rinse with pH-neutral soap and hang to dry.

CUSHION COVER

alder cones

Alder is one of my favourite dyes to work with, and it always surprises me. Sometimes it yields the most beautiful shades of forest green when modified with iron and other times it gives me lively greys. As alders grow abundantly along the riverbanks close to my work, it is an easy dye source for me to access. There are so many different ways to make cushion covers, but this is one of the simplest ways I have tried, and I have tried quite a few!

YOU WILL NEED

TIME: 2½–9½ hrs + 1–5 days soaking alder cones + scouring & mordanting

fabric: 100% Irish linen (use any plant-based fibre you like)

cutting guide: width = cushion insert x 2 + 15 cm (6 in)
height = cushion insert + 2.5 cm (1 in)

dye material: alder cones

how much to use: 2 parts alder : 1 part fibre

mordant: use 1 teaspoon tannin : 100 g (3½ oz) fibre

equipment:
cushion insert
measuring tape
scissors and pins
dye pot with lid
iron for pressing
sewing machine or needle and thread
container for presoaking
sieve
wooden spoon

Alder cones will take a few days of soaking before you extract the colour, so make sure you plan accordingly. Once you have soaked the cones for 1–5 days, it will only take around 1 hour for the dye to extract and then another hour (less for softer shades) for the fabric to take the dye. I would suggest scouring and mordanting your fibre in advance, that way you can go straight into the cutting, sewing and dyeing.

The grey colour shown in the cushions on the opposite page was achieved by mordanting the linen in an iron bath (see page 48) after dyeing in the alder dye.

1. Scour and mordant your linen following the instructions on page 18 and page 24 for scouring and mordanting plant fibres.

2. Measure your cushion insert and note the size. Once your linen is dry, use the cutting guide on page 101 to determine the size needed and cut your linen accordingly.

3. Add the alder cones to the dye pot, cover with boiling water, then cover with a lid and leave to soak for 1–5 days.

4. After letting the cones stand, top up the water until the pot is three-quarters full. Place on the stove and bring to a simmer. Simmer for 1 hour.

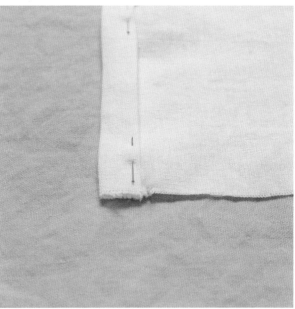

5. Meanwhile, make your cushions. Lay your linen out flat horizontally, wrong side facing you. Turn one of the shorter edges in 5 mm (¼ in) and press in place. Fold in 2 cm (¾ in) and press this in place. Now repeat on the other side.

6. Pin, then stitch both of these edges in place to make two hemmed sides.

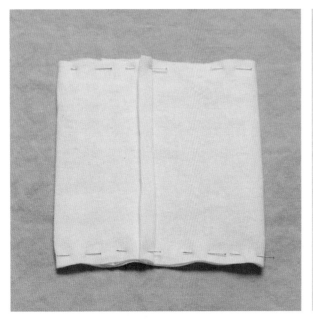

7. Lay your linen out, right side facing up. Fold the right side in, then fold the left on top, so the edges overlap by 10 cm (4 in). Secure along the top and bottom edges with pins. Using a 1 cm (½ in) seam allowance, stitch to close the top edge, then repeat on the bottom. Trim the loose threads.

8. Turn the linen right side out and work out all four corners using your fingers or a narrow, dull object. I like to use the blunt end of a paintbrush. Press the cushion flat, then soak it in a container of water for at least 1–2 hours.

9. Once your dye bath is robust in colour, which may take about 1–2 hours, turn off the heat, leave to cool completely, then strain out all the cones, making sure to strain the dye bath thoroughly.

10. Squeezing out the excess water, add your presoaked cushion cover to the dye, submerging it fully. Return the pot to the stove and bring to a simmer. Simmer for 60 minutes. Turn off the heat and leave the cushion cover in the dye until it takes the colour you like. Remove, rinse in pH-neutral soap and hang to dry.

SILK-DYED BANDANA

This project is a simple one to practise dyeing with tree parts and working with animal fibres. I have used eucalyptus bark, but you can replace the bark with the twigs or nuts from a different tree. As eucalyptus bark is high in tannic acid, mordanting is optional, but I have included it here as a step. The piece requires some sewing to hem the edge of the bandana. If you have never sewn before, you can use a running stitch to tack your hem in place, just make sure to use a thin-headed needle. You will need to prepare your dye bath a few days before dyeing to extract the dye. Plan on presoaking your bark in the dye pot at least 1–3 days ahead of dyeing.

YOU WILL NEED

fabric: 100% silk
1 piece measuring 62 x 62 cm (24 x 24 in)

dye material: eucalyptus bark

how much to use: as animal fibres will take the dye quite intensely, for a rich shade use 2 parts bark : 1 part fibre. For a lighter shade, use equal parts bark to WOF
My silk weighs 25 g (1 oz), so I measured out 50 g (2 oz) of the bark

mordant: mordanting is optional and can be added to increase colour fastness, but it is not required
For animal fibres use 2 teaspoons alum : 100 g (3½ oz) fibre
As my silk weighed 25 g (1 oz), I used ½ teaspoon alum

equipment:
thin-headed needle
scissors and thread
measuring tape
iron for pressing
container for presoaking
dye pot
sieve
wooden spoon

TIME: 3–12 hrs + scouring & mordanting

Scouring and mordanting can be done prior to dyeing. It will take a few days to prepare your dye bath, but the dye only needs 1–2 hours to extract if you have soaked it.

Your stitches do not need to be perfect, especially if you are a novice sewer. Keep them consistent and take your time when stitching.

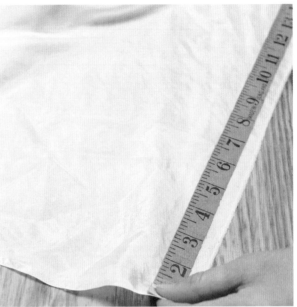

1. Weigh, scour and mordant your fibre following the instructions on pages 20 and 25. Once dry, note the weight, then weigh the corresponding amount of bark. Tear the bark up into pieces, about 7.5–13 cm (3–4½ in) in length. Add to the pot and cover with boiling water. Leave to stand for 1–3 days.

2. When ready to start dyeing, lay your prepared piece of silk on a flat surface and cut out a square measuring 62 × 62 cm (24 × 24 in).

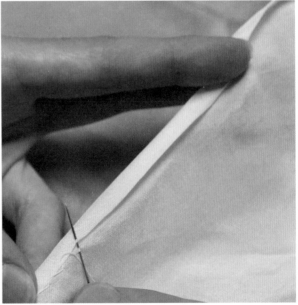

3. Move onto the hem. Measure 5 mm (¼ in) in from the edge, then fold and press in place using an iron. Fold this in another 5 mm (¼ in) and press again. Repeat until all four edges have been pressed in place.

4. Begin your sewing by anchoring your first stitch, then using small, consistent stitches, sew your hem in place. Repeat on the remaining three sides.

5. Once you have hemmed all the edges, presoak your silk in a container of water for 1–2 hours while you prepare your dye bath.

6. Top up the pot containing the soaked bark until it is three-quarters full of water. Place the pot on the heat and simmer for 1–3 hours until there is a change in the colour of the liquid. Turn off the heat, leave to cool completely, then strain out the bark.

7. Squeeze out the excess water from your silk and slowly add to your dye bath. Use the wooden spoon to submerge the fibres fully, working out any air pockets. Return the dye pot to a very gentle heat for 30 minutes, stirring frequently.

8. When your fibre becomes the colour you like, remove the pot from the heat and leave to cool. Squeeze out the excess dye and remove from the pot. For richer colours, leave overnight. Rinse your silk in pH-neutral soap and hang to dry.

BUNDLE DYEING WITH DYE POWDER

Bundle dyeing, also known as eco-printing or eco-dyeing, is a process of wrapping and steaming plant material with fibre to create a variety of beautiful patterns and prints. The dye material is placed on the fibre, folded and wrapped around a stick (or tied in a bundle), then steamed or submerged in water. The heat, in combination with the mordant used, causes the pigment to release and imprint onto the fibre. This is commonly done with flower petals and leaves, but it can also be done using natural dye powders, which are a concentrated form of plant dye, to create strong and vibrant colours.

powder dyes

YOU WILL NEED

TIME: 1 hr 20 mins–2 hrs 10 mins
+ scouring & mordanting

fabric: fibre can be any size. Try experimenting with a few smaller pieces before committing to a larger size. I like to use cloth around 25–75 cm (10–30 in), but you can start with whatever size you want. You can also try this technique on clothing. Here, I have used silk habotai

dye material: look for colours you like:
For yellows & oranges : turmeric, fustic, buckthorn berry, Coreopsis, weld
For purples : logwood
For reds & pinks : madder, Brazilwood
For browns : cutch

how much to use: 1 teaspoon of each dye
1 used 1 teaspoon cutch (brown), 1 teaspoon madder (pinks), 1 teaspoon Brazilwood (reddish pinks), 1 teaspoon turmeric (yellow)

mordant: my fabric had a combined weight of 50 g (2 oz), so I mordanted with 1 teaspoon alum

equipment:
container for presoaking
tea strainer
teaspoon
1 stick for each piece of fibre
string
scissors
dye pot with a lid
a steamer that will fit inside your pot

This technique works best with animal fibres such as silk, but I have also had beautiful results on lightweight linen. The important thing to note here is that the fibre needs to be mordanted before adding the dyes for the colours to stick or bind effectively. You only need a small amount of dye powder to get strong results so keep that in mind when purchasing powder as a little goes a long way. If you like sparse patterning, use less dye and if you want substantial abstract coverage, then use generous amounts of dye powder.

Note: *Make sure your sticks can fit into your pot with the lid on. The length of the sticks should be smaller than the diameter of your pot.*

1. Using scoured, dry fibre, weigh each piece and follow the instructions on page 25 to mordant animal fibres. Once your cloth is mordanted, remove from the solution, rinse and squeeze out the excess liquid.

2. Lay your fibre on a clean surface. You will use the sieve to distribute the powder, just like dusting a cake! Take ½ teaspoon of your chosen dye, slowly place it in the sieve, then carefully dust the powder over the surface of your cloth. Repeat with the remaining colours.

3. Fold your cloth in half, smooth out any wrinkles, then fold it in half again. Place one of your sticks at the narrow end of your cloth and tightly roll the cloth around the stick until it is fully wrapped.

4. Tie a piece of string around the bottom of the cloth and secure it with a knot, then tightly wrap the string around the rest of the cloth and tie in place with a knot. Repeat on all your other pieces of cloth.

5. Place the bundles in a pot with a steamer and fill with water so it is just below the steamer. Be sure to keep your fibres out of the water. Keep the bundles separate and avoid laying them on top of each other. Cover with a lid, place on the stove and heat gently. You want enough heat to create steam but not too much so you boil off the water. Top up the water levels if needed. Steam for 45 minutes for medium shade and 1 hour 30 minutes for stronger tones, turning the bundles at least once. Turn off the heat, uncover and let the fibres cool.

6. Once the bundles are cool enough to touch, remove from the pot, cut the strings and unroll the cloth from the sticks. Handwash each piece separately in cold water with a small amount of eco-friendly detergent. Hang to dry and enjoy your beautiful creations.

DARNING YOUR WOOLLENS

Since returning home to Ireland after more than a decade in California, my blood officially thinned. A wardrobe once filled with light summer layers was quickly replaced with wool – wool socks, jumpers, hats and thermals. When you have so much wool in your life, you inevitably end up with a hole or two in your much-loved socks and jumpers. I think darning your woollens adds character to something already beautiful. There are no hard and fast rules with darning, this is just a guide, so feel free to fill your holes in any way you prefer. I dyed my wool with the dye from olive leaves and the leftover dye from page 79, but dye using any plant you like.

YOU WILL NEED

fibre: 100% wool
I like to use a yarn that is a similar thickness to whatever it is I am darning. If you are mending a thick woollen jumper use a thicker yarn. If you are patching something more delicate like cashmere, consider using a finer thread

dye material: olive leaves
leftover avocado dye from page 79 (optional)

how much to use: 2 parts olive leaves : 1 part fibre for yellow wool
2 parts avocado : 1 part fibre for pink wool
For 100 g (3½ oz) fibre use 200 g (7 oz) olive leaves

mordant: 2 teaspoons alum : 100 g (3½ oz) fibre
I mordanted 100 g (3½ oz) wool in 2 teaspoons alum

equipment:
container for presoaking
dye pot
wooden spoon
sieve
darning egg (or a small ball/tennis ball will work if you don't have a darning egg)
darning needle
scissors

TIME: 11 hrs + 1–3 days soaking olive leaves + scouring & mordanting + 1 day to wash wool

You will need to scour, mordant and presoak your wool before dyeing. You will also need to prepare your olive leaves by leaving them to soak for a few days before extracting the dye. Once you extract the dye, you will need to let it cool overnight before adding your wool to the liquid. I find it helpful to scour and mordant a few skeins of wool at a time, so I always have some ready. When darning, I like to work with the right side facing me. A lot of instructions tell you to turn your knit inside out but quite often that leaves you with an open area on the front when you are done.

A note on darning: Darning is like weaving, you weave or sew your stitches up and down vertically until the hole or spot is covered with stitches, then the stitches are weaved horizontally through, picking up every other stitch until you get to the end of the row. The next row is done weaving through but picking up the opposite stitches to the previous row. You repeat this until your hole is covered.

1. Following the instructions on page 64 for dyeing with olive leaves, prepare the leaves by cutting them up as much as possible, then add them to the dye pot, cover with boiling water and leave to soak for 1–3 days.

2. Place the dye pot on the stove, fill three-quarters full with water and bring to the boil. Reduce the heat and simmer for 1–2 hours. Once the dye is robust in colour, turn off the heat, leave to cool overnight, then strain out all the leaves.

3. To estimate the right amount for a darning project, I take a piece of wool and wrap it around my hand 15 times. This is always more than enough, but it also ensures I don't run out.

4. Following the instructions on page 20 and page 25 for scouring and mordanting animal fibres, scour and mordant your wool. Place your wool in a container of water and leave to soak while you prepare and cool the dye bath.

5. You will now have two dye baths: one olive and one leftover avocado. Divide the scoured, mordanted and presoaked wool between the dye baths, making sure to submerge it completely and leave the yarn until you are happy with the colour. Leave overnight for stronger colours.

6. Remove your yarn from the dye pot and use a pH-neutral soap to gently rinse thoroughly (do not scrub or agitate your yarn as it may felt). Hang to dry.

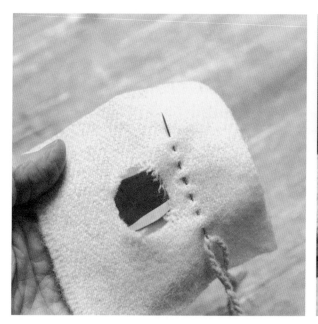

7. Selecting one of your dyed yarns, begin your darning. Turn your piece inside out and clean up any loose thread or fibre. If you can salvage any stitches by tying loose threads together, do so. Turn your piece so the right side is facing you and place the darning egg under the hole. Begin your first stitch. Don't pull the yarn through all the way, instead leave 5–7.5 cm (2–3 in) loose (we will tidy this up at the end).

8. Begin your stitches with a running stitch around the diameter of the hole. Stitch up and down until the hole is covered with vertical stitches.

9. Going horizontally, weave your yarn over the first row of stitches, picking up every other stitch until you have covered your hole.

10. On the next row, weave your yarn through, picking up the opposite stitches. Repeat until your hole is covered.

11. To tidy up the tail ends of your first and last stitch, weave the stitches 2.5–5 cm (1–2 in) into the surrounding fibre, then snip your loose threads.

BOJAGI-INSPIRED CLOTH

avocado

Bojagi, or pojagi, is a traditional type of Korean cloth used to wrap gifts, present marriage proposals, protect heirlooms, cover food or as tablecloths. Traditionally, they were made from pieces of silk sewn together, but ramie or hemp were also commonly used. I made this using lightweight sheer linen, dyed with avocado, tea and a combination of avocado and tea, which work beautifully together. It is a simple project, but it does take time so don't rush. It is a beautiful piece to make to gift wrap something for someone you love.

YOU WILL NEED

TIME: 3¾–10¼ hrs + scouring & mordanting

fabric: 100% lightweight sheer linen
I used a piece of linen measuring 69 x 58 cm (27 x 23 in) which weighed 45 g (1¾ oz)
You can use any sheer fabric you like; silk works beautifully

dye material: avocado stones, black tea

how much to use: 1 part black tea : 1 part fibre
2 parts avocado stones : 1 part fibre

mordant: 1 teaspoon tannin : 100 g (3½ oz) fibre

equipment:
2 x dye pots
wooden spoon
container for presoaking
sieve
needle and thread or sewing machine
scissors
iron for pressing

Although the fabric is quick to dye, it will take time to sew the pieces together. It is well worth the time and effort as the end result is so beautiful. This is the kind project you could pick up after a long day, as it is quite meditative to sew.

1. Scour and mordant your piece following the instructions on page 18 and page 24. When dry, weigh and note the weight. Set up two dye pots. Weigh your avocado and tea separately, then follow the instructions on page 58 and page 56 for dyeing with avocado and black tea.

2. Meanwhile, lay your prepared linen flat on a surface and cut it into five different sized pieces, then presoak it in a container of water for 1–2 hours while you prepare your dye baths. When the dye baths are ready, turn off the heat, leave to cool completely, then strain out all the stones and leaves.

3. Dye two pieces in avocado for different amounts of time, so that one piece is relatively darker than the first (I cannot tell you how long as this part is up to you). Dye three pieces in black tea for various lengths of time (again this is up to you).

4. After the pieces have been in the black tea for at least 10 minutes (or longer if you like), remove one piece, rinse it thoroughly, then add it to the avocado bath and leave it in for as long as you want.

5. Remove all five pieces of linen from the dye baths, rinse and hang to dry. Lightly press each piece. You should have two pieces of avocado-dyed linen in two different shades, two pieces of black tea in two different shades and one piece of linen dyed with a combination of avocado and tea, giving you five different hues.

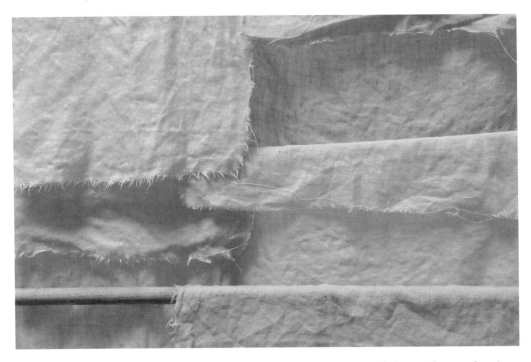

6. Think about the overall design of your piece and feel free to sketch some possible layouts. Cut your five pieces of linen into smaller pieces that you will then rearrange and sew back together. Consider placing contrasting hues side by side.

7. Take two pieces of linen and place one on top of the other, right sides facing. Offset the top piece, so it is 5 mm (¼ in) in from the edge of the bottom piece, and pin in place.

8. With a 5 mm (¼ in) seam allowance, use a simple running stitch to sew the top piece in place.

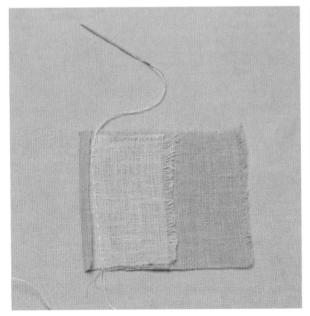

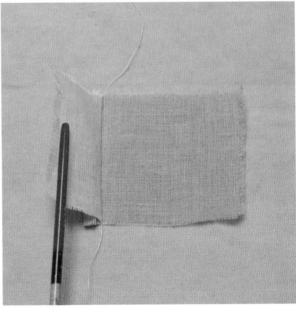

9. Fold the outer edge in to meet the stitch line and use the iron to press in place.

10. Open the top piece, so it lies over the stitching you just did, then use the iron to press this seam open.

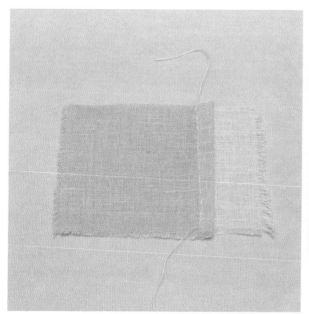
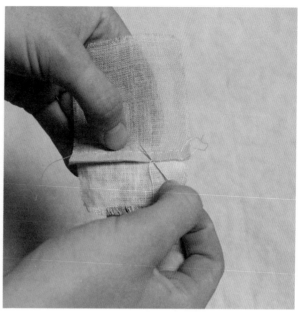

11. Turn this piece over and use simple, consistent stitches to sew the folded edge down. Both pieces are now secured together.

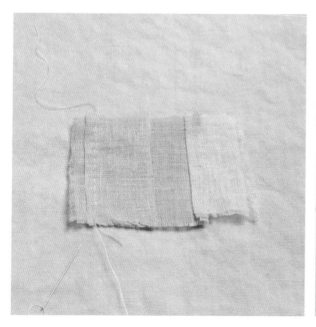

12. To add your next piece, lay your linen right sides facing together, offset by 5 mm (¼ in), then pin this in place. Using a 5 mm (¼ in) seam allowance, stitch in place, then fold the outer edge in to meet the stitch line. Press, turn over and press the new seam open. Turn back around and stitch the folded hem down. Take your time to repeat this sequence until you have sewn all your pieces together.

EASY

WATERCOLOUR PAINT

You can easily make your own natural watercolour paints from your leftover dye baths. It is a great way to experiment with modifiers and see how they affect whichever dye you choose to work with. Consider setting up small modifiers with vinegar, lemon juice, bicarbonate of soda (baking soda), soda ash or perhaps some iron water. This recipe is made using condensed plant dyes mixed with a water-soluble binder. I used a glutinous rice flour, but you can try using starch flour, such as cornflour or potato flour. You can also try using gum Arabic as a binder if you don't have any flour.

leftover dyes

YOU WILL NEED

binder: starch binder (glutenous rice flour, cornflour, potato flour or gum Arabic)

how much to use: for the binder 120 ml (4 fl oz/½ cup) water :
1 teaspoon glutenous rice flour
If using gum Arabic, add 10 drops : 60 ml (2 fl oz/¼ oz) reduced dye

paper: 1 sheet of watercolour paper or handmade cotton paper

dye material: leftover dye bath

how much to use: at least 120 ml (4 fl oz/½ cup) dye

equipment:
small dye pot
wooden spoon
measuring jug
bowl
whisk
tablespoon
paintbrush

TIME: 30 mins–1 hr

The beautiful thing about this recipe is that it is incredibly easy to make. All you need is some leftover dye, a binder, heat and some patience. The key to making beautiful watercolours is to condense or reduce the liquid down as much as possible. Once it is reduced, it is mixed with a binder, heated a little more, then left to cool. If you have your dye bath already made you can make paints in less than an hour.

1. Measure 120 ml (4 fl oz/½ cup) dye (a little more or less is OK) and add this to a small dye pot. Place on the heat and simmer the dye, reducing it as much as possible. You want it to reduce without evaporating it completely. The more concentrated, the better.

2. Meanwhile, prepare the binder by mixing 120 ml (4 fl oz/½ cup) water with 1 teaspoon glutinous rice flour in a bowl. Use a whisk to dissolve the flour thoroughly.

3. Mix 2 tablespoons of the reduced dye with 1 tablespoon of the binder. If you want more watercolour paint, add more at this ratio.

4. Place this solution on the heat and simmer for a few minutes until it condenses again. I can't tell you exactly how long to heat it for, but you are aiming for a nicely reduced dye liquid. Once the liquid has evaporated slightly, remove from the heat and leave to cool. Your watercolour is now ready to use.

137

Suppliers & Resources

Below is a list of suppliers for natural dyes, mordants, fibres, fabric and haberdashery that I have used in my studio or have come recommended to me.

UK & Europe

Fibres, fabric, natural dyes, mordants, etc.

AppleOak FibreWorks; www.appleoakfibreworks.com
George Weil; www.georgeweil.com
Wild Colours; www.wildcolours.co.uk

Irish linen

Emblem Weavers, Ireland; www.emblemweavers.com

Organic & natural fabrics & yarn

Bristol Cloth; www.bristolcloth.co.uk
Greenfibres; www.greenfibres.com
Organic Textile Company; www.organiccotton.biz

Sewing supplies, scissors and haberdashery

Merchant & Mills; www.merchantandmills.com

North America

Fabric, fibres, natural dyes, mordants, etc.

Aurora Silk; www.aurorasilk.com/wp/
A Verb for Keeping Warm; www.averbforkeepingwarm.com
Botanical Colours; www.botanicalcolors.com
Dharma Trading Company; www.dharmatrading.com
Fabrics-store.com; www.fabrics-store.com
Maiwa Handprints; www.maiwa.com

For naturally dyed textiles and workshops visit Kathryn Davey; www.kathryndavey.com
info@kathryndavey.com

Acknowledgements

My heartfelt thanks go to everyone involved in the making of this book. To the excellent team at Marabout, especially Catie Ziller for presenting me with the opportunity to write this book. Catie, thank you for appreciating my work and for trusting in me to bring this to life. Thank you for your patience and easy way with me throughout the process. Alice Chadwick, I'm incredibly grateful to you for all your elegant design work, for translating the text and imagery onto the pages in such a beautiful way and for all the kind emails along the way. Kathy Steer, thank you for making my words make sense and for your patient and gentle correspondence throughout the completion of this book.

My darling daughters, Alannah, Kaijsa and Rose, I know things haven't been easy for us. Thank you for seeing the value in my work. Thanks for your love and respect; I couldn't be prouder of each of you than I am. Tim, thank you for being my greatest champion, for always saying 'you've got this' especially when I feel like I don't. Thank you for all the love and support (especially the dinners) while I burrowed my head in the making of this book. Mum, thanks for all your help with gathering and collecting dye plants. You and Dad have been such consistent examples of creativity, I am forever indebted to you both. Doreen, your work is a constant source of inspiration. Thank you for your beautiful eye and images that have made this book what it is. I am so grateful to you for being a part of these pages and for generously sharing your knowledge and camera with me, thank you.

Kaijsa, thank you for gathering plant materials in the rain. For being the most beautiful hand model while holding the most awkward of positions. Thank you for your easy, gentle, beautiful and bright presence in the studio and everything you have done to help me with this book. To my dearest friend, Daragh, there are no words of gratitude for all the years of friendship, thank you. Fergal, thanks for indulging my random requests for onion skins and for holding onto them even when they began to smell! Masha, thank you for encouraging me to write and for providing a platform on which to share. Thank you for the kindest encouragement and our new found friendship. Liz, thank you for helping me navigate these last few years, your help has been invaluable and so appreciated. I will forever be grateful to you. To Kelsey and Ros, thank you for such nurturing friendship and consistent, unwavering support. To all the natural dyers who graciously share what they know with others. To Kathy Hatori for instilling me with the confidence to naturally dye and sharing your knowledge so freely. To Jenny Dean, whose book *Wild Colours* was my first guide into this beautiful world of colour. For Wendy at Scout, thank you for your support over these last few years, it's been such a pleasure to work with you. A huge thanks to Morgan and Zoe at Homestudios, I often spend more time at work than at home and you have made HS a refuge from this crazy world.

Lastly, thank you to all the wonderful people that have attended my workshops and purchased my naturally dyed goods. You have made it possible for me to continue to do this work that I love so much. A huge thanks for all the kind messages of encouragement and continued support. Without you, none of this would be possible.

Index

Entries in italics refer to the project names.

Index

W

Y

This edition published in 2022 by Hardie Grant Books, an imprint of Hardie Grant Publishing

First published in 2021 by Hachette Livre (Marabout).
© Hachette Livre (Marabout) 2021

Hardie Grant Books (London)
5th & 6th Floors
52–54 Southwark Street
London SE1 1UN

Hardie Grant Books (Melbourne)
Building 1, 658 Church Street
Richmond, Victoria 3121
hardiegrantbooks.com

The moral rights of the author have been asserted. British Library Cataloguing-in-Publication Data. A catalogue record for this book is available from the British Library.

Natural Dyeing
ISBN: 9781784884949
10 9 8 7 6 5 4 3 2 1

For Marabout
Publisher: Catie Ziller
Author: Kathryn Davey
Photographers: Doreen Kilfeather & Kathryn Davey
Design: Alice Chadwick
Editor: Kathy Steer

For Hardie Grant
Publisher: Kajal Mistry
Design: Studio Noel
Proofreader: René Nel
Production controller: Nikolaus Ginelli

Colour reprodution by p2d
Printed and bound in China by Leo Paper Products Ltd.

MIX
Paper from responsible sources
FSC™ C020056
www.fsc.org